Year 2/P3

TEACHER'S RESOURCE BOOK

Louis Fidge and Christine Moorcroft

STANLEY
THORNES

STANLEY THORNES

CHELTENHAM

Acknowledgements: 'The End of the Road', © Hilaire Belloc, reprinted by permission of The Peters Fraser and Dunlop Group Limited on behalf of *The Estate of Hilaire Belloc*. Christian (Anglican) wedding, material from *Alternative Services, First Series: Solemnisation of Matrimony* is copyright © The Central Board of Finance of the Church of England and is reproduced by permission.

Poster illustrations: *Harvest Festival,* John Crawford Fraser; *A Shared Meal,* Central Gurdwara, Shepherds Bush, Martin Sookias; *Weddings,* John Crawford Fraser; *Wesak,* Jane Taylor; *The Mu'adhin,* Jane Taylor; *Guru Nanak,* Carlos Reyes-Manzo, Andes Press Agency; *The Buddha,* Topham Picturepoint; *A Stone Circle,* Calanais Standing Stones, Isle of Lewis, © Crown copyright, Historic Scotland; *A Place for Prayer,* the Garden of Gethsemane, Jane Taylor; *Cathedral,* Liverpool Cathedral, R J L Smith and Associates; *Synagogue,* Cheltenham Synagogue, Martin Sookias; *Doorways,* Wayland Picture Library/Tim Woodcock, Steve White-Thomson.

First published in 1997 by
Stanley Thornes Publishers Ltd
Ellenborough House
Wellington Street
Cheltenham
GL50 1YW

97 98 99 00 \ 10 9 8 7 6 5 4 3 2 1

A catalogue record for this book is available from the British Library

ISBN 0-7487-3043-5

Designed by Penny Mills.
Illustrated by Chris Masters.

Printed and bound in Great Britain by
Redwood Books, Trowbridge, Wiltshire

Contents

Introduction 4

Unit 1 Special Times 8

Unit 2 Special People. 30

Unit 3 Special Places 52

Poems, Songs and Prayers 78

Stories 80

Extra Background Information 93

Introduction

Stanley Thornes Infant RE provides a complete, self-contained, structured programme for teaching religious education throughout Years 1 and 2/P2 and 3.

The scheme is based on the recommendations of the School Curriculum and Assessment Authority (SCAA) (1994) and is compatible with locally agreed syllabuses and the Scottish 5–14 guidelines. It complies with the Education Reform Act (1988) which requires that religious education should '...reflect the fact that the religious traditions in Great Britain are in the main Christian, while taking account of teachings and practices of other principal religions represented in Great Britain ...'. Following SCAA recommendations the six faiths addressed are: Buddhism, Christianity, Hinduism, Islam, Judaism and Sikhism, with the emphasis on Christianity. It takes into account the fact that most infant schools will choose which of these faiths to include and give priority to in their religious education schemes.

In addition to learning about religions the scheme offers opportunities to learn from religions; this supports the promotion of children's spiritual, moral and cultural development.

To help non-specialist teachers and to save the teacher's time the relevant background information for each religious topic is always provided, as are stories, poems, songs and prayers, where appropriate.

Stanley Thornes Infant RE is designed to help pupils to:

◆ develop knowledge and understanding of Christianity and the other main religions of Great Britain;

◆ understand the ways in which beliefs, values and traditions influence people, communities and culture;

◆ use the teachings of the major faiths to inform thoughtful judgements about religious and moral issues;

◆ develop social, moral, cultural and spiritual awareness by:

  • becoming aware of the fundamental questions of life which are raised by the experiences of people and considering them in the light of religious teachings;
  • in considering these questions, referring to the teachings and practices of the religions which they have studied;
  • thinking about their own beliefs, values and experiences against the background of their learning about different religions;

◆ become increasingly positive in their attitudes towards others, being able to respect their beliefs and values and develop the ability to live in a multi-faith society.

The introduction to each unit shows the religious focus of each lesson and gives an overview of how the six major faiths are addressed. Reflecting the way in which religious education is taught in most infant schools, the approach of the scheme is topic-based, with many opportunities for discussion of 'general' topics which are not tied to just one religion, for example, personal identity, family and celebrating. It recognises that many schools address the Christian festivals, Christmas and Easter, each year; these appear in both Books 1 and 2, but with built-in progression, enabling teachers to build on and develop from the children's previous learning.

As required by the Education Reform Act (1988) the scheme presents religious education in a way which supports teachers in developing children's understanding of different faiths without attempting to inculcate a particular religious belief in the children. It recognises that the children who learn from it, and their teachers, are from a range of faith backgrounds or none at all.

TERMINOLOGY

The terminology used in *Stanley Thornes Infant RE* is in line with the specific spellings and usages recommended by SCAA. However, there may be local variations to these and schools will need to be sensitive to local and regional conventions. In all the pupils' material, and on the first mention in the teacher's material, the name of the Prophet Muhammad is followed by the initials 'pbuh'. This is the written abbreviation of the words 'Peace be upon him', which are always spoken after Muhammad's name by Muslims, as a mark of respect. Again, schools will need to be sensitive to this practice, and also to any variations of this phrase which may be in use locally.

ORGANISATION

Stanley Thornes Infant RE provides two 112-page teacher's books, each of which is supported by 12 full-colour posters. It is appreciated that no published scheme can possibly address the individual needs of every school. With this in mind, the books are designed to be as flexible as possible. The units may be interchanged with one another; the lessons within each unit are self-contained, and so the sequence of lessons may be altered to suit the needs of the school. The scheme takes account of the fact that some schools have mixed-age classes; the differentiated learning outcomes are particularly useful in these schools. They are also intended to encourage teachers to develop each child's learning to the full.

Each book is organised into three units (one per term), followed by a resources section which offers stories and additional background information. Each unit has a brief introduction setting out its contents and indicating its intended learning outcomes.

STANLEY THORNES

infant RE

Year 1/ P2	Year 2/ P3
Myself	Special Times
New Life	Special People
Special Books	Special Places

A unit consists of ten one-hour 'lessons' (easily divisible into shorter pieces), each of which consists of lesson plan notes faced by a photocopy sheet. The teacher's pages have been designed to facilitate ease of use, with clear and consistent headings.

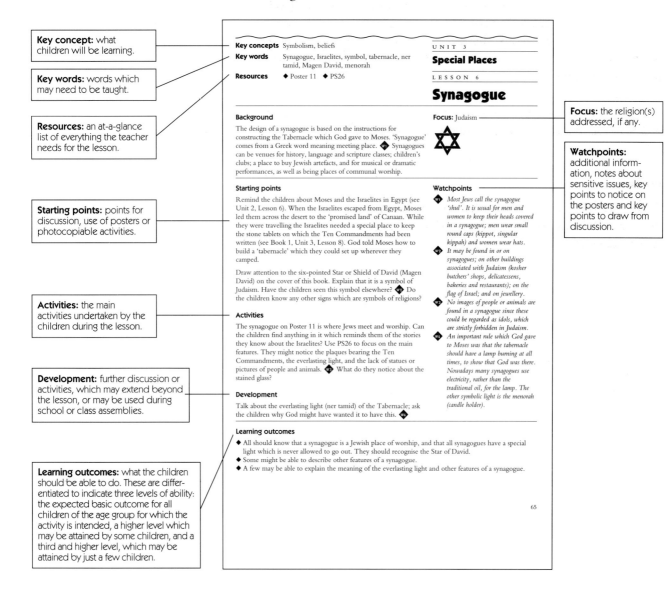

Key concept: what children will be learning.

Key words: words which may need to be taught.

Resources: an at-a-glance list of everything the teacher needs for the lesson.

Starting points: points for discussion, use of posters or photocopiable activities.

Activities: the main activities undertaken by the children during the lesson.

Development: further discussion or activities, which may extend beyond the lesson, or may be used during school or class assemblies.

Learning outcomes: what the children should be able to do. These are differentiated to indicate three levels of ability: the expected basic outcome for all children of the age group for which the activity is intended, a higher level which may be attained by some children, and a third and higher level, which may be attained by just a few children.

Focus: the religion(s) addressed, if any.

Watchpoints: additional information, notes about sensitive issues, key points to notice on the posters and key points to draw from discussion.

ASSESSMENT AND RECORDING

England and Wales

The 'end of Key Stage statements of attainment' suggested by SCAA are adopted here as the criteria by which children's learning should be assessed:

Learning about religions (AT1)
Pupils recognise and describe people, objects, symbols, places and events encountered [in the programme of study], and remember the outlines of stories. They talk or write about a religion, or an aspect of

religion, linking some of the key people, objects, places and events. They identify the religions to which these belong, and show awareness that some features, for example festivals, are characteristic of more than one religion. They suggest meanings for religious symbols, stories and language: for example, God as Father.

Learning from religion (AT2)
Pupils respond to spiritual or religious aspects of stories in the light of their own experience and thoughts. They show understanding that some questions in life are difficult to answer. They recognise good and bad examples set by characters in stories and by those around them. They show awareness that some things are right and some are wrong, and relate the moral issues encountered in their daily lives to religious teachings.

The learning outcomes of each lesson are linked to these statements and provide a basis for completing the photocopiable Pupil Record Sheet (page 101).

Scotland

'Learning about religions', above, equates to the 5-14 attainment outcomes 'Christianity' and 'Other World Religions'.
'Learning from religion', above, equates to the 5-14 'Personal Search'.

Special Times

INTRODUCTION

This Unit begins by inviting children to remember their own special times: what made them special, what they and others did and how they and others felt. It introduces the idea of celebration linked to events, and of the regular recurrence of festivals.

Joyful family celebrations such as birthdays are featured: the preparation, rituals, symbols, gifts, food, decorations, clothes and cards. The observance of other milestones in the life of an individual, such as naming and marriage, is explored, as well as that of community festivals such as Wesak, Divali, Hanukkah, Id ul-Fitr and Advent. The seasonal celebration of harvest is explored, with the emphasis on giving thanks.

The lessons in this Unit encourage the children to appreciate the significance of a range of special times to individuals and to communities.

The symbols of celebrations are explored: their origins and meanings and the ways in which they are used.

Unit 1 – Overview

Lesson	Contents	Key Concepts	Religious Focus
1	**Milestones** The main themes of the lesson are marking special occasions and the feeling of celebration: ◆ Special occasions in families and how we celebrate them. ◆ Rites of passage. ◆ Special times in an individual's life.	Lifestyle, beliefs and values	General
2	**Harvest** The Parable of the Sower is used to introduce the Christian idea of God's harvest of people: ◆ What things are we thankful for? ◆ Whom would we thank for them and how? ◆ Giving thanks to God. ◆ Harvest festival.	Lifestyle, beliefs and values	Christianity
3	**A Shared Meal** In most major religions sharing with others is important: ◆ Experiences of sharing. ◆ The sharing of a meal in a Sikh langar. ◆ The emphasis on equality.	Lifestyle, beliefs and values	Sikhism

Lesson	Contents	Key Concepts	Religious Focus
4	**Names and Threads** There are many ways in which babies' names are chosen: ♦ The naming ceremony for a Hindu baby. ♦ The symbolism of threads in Hinduism.	Symbolism, belonging	Hinduism
5	**Wedding** All religious traditions have wedding ceremonies: ♦ Our experiences of weddings. ♦ The meanings of the symbols used during them. ♦ A Sikh and a Christian wedding. ♦ The promises which a bride and groom make to one another.	Symbolism, belonging	Christianity/ Sikhism
6	**Wesak** Wesak commemorates the life of the Buddha: ♦ The way the festival is celebrated. ♦ The meaning of the festival. ♦ Our deeds of the past year and resolutions for the next year.	Symbolism, belonging, beliefs and values	Buddhism
7	**Divali** The story of Rama and Sita is very important in Hinduism: ♦ Good and evil characters in this and other stories. ♦ The ways in which the festival is celebrated. ♦ The customs and symbolism.	Belonging	Hinduism
8	**Hanukkah** Hanukkah is a very important Jewish Festival: ♦ The hanukiah (the nine-branched candle holder with its candles). ♦ The story of Judas Maccabeus. ♦ The symbolism of the candles. ♦ How Hanukkah is celebrated. ♦ A traditional Hanukkah dreidl game.	Symbolism, belonging	Judaism
9	**Id ul-Fitr** Many religions have a tradition of fasting: ♦ What is our experience of fasting? ♦ The importance to Muslims of fasting during Ramadan. ♦ The idea of feasting and joyfulness after the fast. ♦ How do we feel while waiting for a special event?	Commitment, belonging, lifestyle	Islam
10	**Advent** This begins by considering the preparation for any important event, including all the special things which people do only for such an occasion: ♦ The ways, both religious and secular, in which Christians prepare for Christmas. ♦ The symbols of Christmas and Advent. ♦ For Christians, Advent commemorates the preparation for the coming of Jesus.	Belonging, beliefs	Christianity

Birthday Symbols

Find the birthday things.

Draw something
which reminds you
of birthdays.

Key concepts Lifestyle, beliefs and values

Key words Commemorate, event, celebrate

Resources ◆ PS1

Milestones

Background

Focus General

Most religions have events to mark the passing from one phase in life to the next. Hinduism has samskars (ceremonies which mark events such as birth, naming, marriage, death, etc.). Islam has simpler celebrations of rites of passage: birth, marriage and death. Other celebrations include: Ordination in Buddhism, Confirmation or First Communion in Christianity, Bar Mitzvah/Bat Mitzvah (Son of/Daughter of Commandment) in Judaism and the Khalsa (taking Amrit) in Sikhism.

Starting points

Ask the children to think of special events in their own lives. Name any which happen regularly. Ask what a birthday means and why it is celebrated on the same date each year.

Activities

Ask the children to draw pictures of birthday celebrations. Are there special clothes, food, drink, etc.? What other special things are there? Talk about the children's feelings before, during and after a birthday party. Are there other ways to celebrate a birthday? Make a graph to record them. Which is the most popular?

Use PS1 to introduce symbols associated with birthdays. The children should identify them and then draw and label some of their own.

Development

Talk about milestones in the children's lives. At what age were they able to do certain things? They could make personal time-lines or scrapbooks to show these milestones.

They could take turns to talk about special times for other people (e.g. when they began at a new school or a new job, when they moved house) or display photos or cards which mark milestones.

Watchpoints

W1 *Some Muslims and Jehovah's Witnesses might not celebrate birthdays.*

Learning outcomes

◆ All should be able to talk about ways to celebrate birthdays and name or draw some of the associated symbols. They should know that birthdays are celebrated only once a year and why this is.

◆ Some may be able to describe other milestones in people's lives.

◆ A few may be able to distinguish between personal milestones (e.g. birth, wedding) and annual community commemorations.

Thank You

I am thankful for:

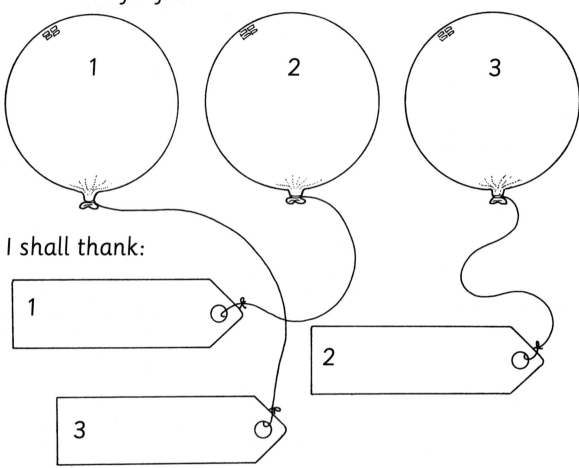

I shall thank:

This is how I shall thank them:

Key concepts Lifestyle, beliefs and values

Key words Crops, parable, thank you, harvest festival

Resources ◆ Poster 1 ◆ PS2 ◆ Hymn (page 79)
◆ Story 'The Parable of the Sower' (page 80)

Harvest

Background

Most religions have seasonal celebrations such as the harvest, first fruits, New Year or the end of the rainy season. Christian harvest festivals take place in autumn in Britain. The children may know secular, seasonal, community celebrations (e.g. local carnivals, Well-Dressing in Derbyshire, the Flower Festival in Jersey).

Focus: Christianity

Starting points

Ask the children to name things for which they have said 'Thank you'. Record their responses. Whom did they thank? Can they think of other ways to say 'Thank you'? **W1**

Ask what Poster 1 shows. Why are harvest festivals in the autumn? Talk about the farming year: what worries might farmers have before the harvest and how might they feel when the crops are ready? Why do Christians take foods into a church at harvest time? **W2**

Activities

The children could make thank you cards. Whom do they want to thank? For what? Ask them what Christians thank God for at harvest festivals. They could draw and label these things. Read the extract from 'We Plough the Fields' (page 79) and ask what people who sing it are thanking God for and what they can give him as a 'thank you'.

When completing PS2 the children should choose the three most important things for which they want to say thank you.

Development

Read the Parable of the Sower (page 80). Ask what it says about the care which a sower must take when sowing seeds. **W3**

What should the sower do when harvesting the grain so that there is some seed to plant the following year? What other gifts from God do people use in careful/careless ways (e.g. water, air, energy)?

Talk about stories with meanings: Jesus meant not only that some of the good seeds scattered by sowers would fail but that the seeds were like the words of God: some people would take notice of them but some would not.

Watchpoints

W1 *Responses might include: writing a letter, sending a thank you card, giving a present, smiling, hugging, kissing.*

W2 *In the past it was not possible to buy certain foods all year round, and most people could only buy what was harvested locally. If the harvest failed there could be a famine and they might starve. The same applies in some developing countries today.*

W3 *Make sure the children do not confuse 'sow' with 'sew'.*

Learning outcomes

◆ All should be able to describe how a church is decorated for harvest festival. They should know that harvest festivals are for thanking God for his provision, and be able to re-tell the Parable of the Sower.

◆ Some may be able to say what Christians thank God for and what they can do to be sure of a good harvest.

◆ A few may be able to describe the meaning of the Parable of the Sower.

A Meal to Share

Draw and label your favourite meals.

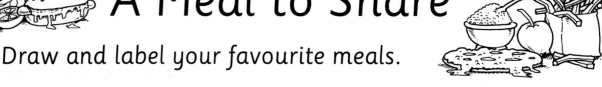

1	2

3	4

Ask the children in your group which meals they would like to eat with you.

Name	Meal (✓ or ✗)			
	1	2	3	4

Key concepts Lifestyle, beliefs and values

Key words Gurdwara, langar, share, equal

Resources ◆ Poster 2 ◆ PS3

A Shared Meal

Background

A gurdwara (temple) always has a langar, which is a free kitchen where a meal is served after the religious service. When people eat in the langar it is considered an act of religious merit, since it shows that they regard themselves as the equals of all others who eat there. Volunteers take turns to pay for and cook the meals, to which anyone is welcome, whatever their religion.

Focus: Sikhism

Starting points

Ask the children to name some things they share (e.g. sweets, fruit, crisps). Record and discuss their responses. Do they share these equally among their friends or do they just offer one or two? How do they decide with whom they will share? How would they feel if everything they brought to school had to be shared with the whole class? If they would object, ask why. Should some have more because they brought more? Is that fair?

Show Poster 2. What are the people sharing? Where are the people sitting? Do any of them look more important than others or do all look equally important? **W1** What else do the children notice about the people? **W2**

Activities

Use PS3 to plan a meal for the class to share. They need to find out about other children's likes and dislikes, and which foods they cannot eat for religious, medical or ethical reasons. They should find a fair way to decide who should pay for the meal and an effective way of sharing the work of preparing it.

After looking at and discussing Poster 2 the children could draw and write about the shared meal, describing anything special which they notice about it or the people sharing it.

Development

Talk about the sharing of food during and after worship. **W3** Do the children go to a place of worship where food is shared?

Watchpoints

W1 *They are sharing food. There is no 'top table' and everyone is seated at the same level, even if this is on the floor. Guru Nanak, the founder of Sikhism, stressed that all people are equally important, whatever their race, caste, religion or wealth.*

W2 *Many of the men are wearing turbans, the boys have long hair tied on top of their heads, and the women and girls have long hair.*

W3 *As in a Hindu temple, karah parshad (sweet food) is distributed in the Sikh gurdwara at the end of formal worship. The ingredients are stirred with a kirpan (sword), and a prayer, the Japji Sahib, is recited.*

Learning outcomes

◆ All should be able to describe the shared meal in a Sikh langar, noting that volunteers take turns to pay for and prepare it. They should know that karah parshad is a special food which is made sacred by blessing and then shared.

◆ Some may be able to explain the significance of sharing a meal after worship: that sharing helps people to feel part of a group or family.

◆ A few may be able to say how the meal makes all the people who share it equal.

Favourite Names

| A B C D E F G H I J K L M |
| N O P Q R S T U V W X Y Z |

Choose a letter.

Write it in this box.

What are your favourite names beginning
with this letter?

boy

girl

I like this name

because ———————————————

————————————————————

————————————————————

————————————————————

I like this name

because ———————————————

————————————————————

————————————————————

————————————————————

Key concepts Symbolism, belonging

Key words Aum, thread

Resources ◆ PS4 ◆ Red and black embroidery thread
or wool

Names and Threads

Background

Most religions have rituals for welcoming a new baby into the faith.
Namskara, the name-giving ceremony, is practised by many Hindus.
A priest might prepare a horoscope which indicates the initial letter
or a syllable to be included. The choice might be influenced by
family names or favourite deities. The name-giving ceremony
sometimes takes place at home, but more often in the temple. **W1**

Focus: Hinduism

Starting points

Ask the children if they know how their names were chosen.
Why do parents sometimes name a baby after a relation or friend?
W2 Whose name would the children choose for a new baby in
their family? Why?

Explain that Hindu mothers often tie a thread around the baby's
wrist. What is this for? **W3**

Explain also that when a baby is born in a Hindu family someone
will often write the aum symbol with honey on the baby's
tongue. **W4**

Activities

PS4 asks the children to choose a letter and write their favourite
names beginning with that letter. Why do they like those names?

Do the children wear or carry anything for luck? They could
draw and describe it. How would they feel if they lost it? They
could do a survey to find out about other people's 'lucky things'.

Development

Ask the children what wishes they would make for a baby. They
could make twisted threads to put around the wrists of dolls.

They could draw pictures to show how they would welcome a
new baby. What interests would they like the baby to have in the
future? How could they help him or her in these interests?

Watchpoints

W1 *Lists of Hindu names may be
obtained from some Hindu temples.*

W2 *Responses might be: because it is a
family tradition; to please someone;
because they hope the child will be
like him/her; they want him/her to
be the child's friend; because they
are fond of the person.*

W3 *Many Hindu mothers tie bright red
and black threads around their
babies' wrists and on their cradles
for luck and to keep away evil.*

W4 *'Aum' is the most sacred sound in
Hinduism, believed by many to be
the sound which was made as the
world was being created.*

Learning outcomes

◆ All should be able to describe how a Hindu baby's name is chosen. They should know that the baby
might have a thread tied around the wrist for good luck.

◆ Some will be able to discuss things carried for good luck and what effect they might have.

◆ A few might be able to explain some of the ways in which babies, particularly Hindu babies, are
welcomed into the world and how adults try to influence their developing characters.

Wedding

Draw a Christian wedding and a Sikh wedding.

| **A Christian wedding** | **A Sikh wedding** |

Match the symbols to the weddings.

rings

Sikh

bunch of flowers

garlands

chuni

Christian

white dress

red clothes

Key concepts	Symbolism, belonging
Key words	Wedding, marry, symbolise, responsibility
Resources	◆ Poster 3 ◆ PS5 ◆ Information about weddings (page 93) ◆ Christian and/or Sikh wedding video

Wedding

Background

A Christian wedding takes place in a church or chapel, conducted by a priest or minister, and the bride and bridegroom promise to live together as partners until they die.

A Sikh wedding, Anand Karaj (ceremony of bliss), can be performed anywhere, in the presence of the Guru Granth Sahib (holy book), but usually takes place in a gurdwara, followed by a meal in the langar. The ceremony can be led by any Sikh.

Focus: Christianity, Sikhism

Starting points

Ask the children to describe weddings which they have attended. What did the bride and groom wear? What did they say during the service? What happened after the service?

Discuss the two weddings on Poster 3. Can the children identify the bride and groom in each one?

Focus on the Sikh wedding. Draw attention to the chuni (scarf) which joins the bride and groom together. Can they explain this?

Activities

Read the questions from the Christian (Anglican) marriage service (page 94) and ask the children why they are asked.

If possible show a video of a Christian and/or Sikh wedding. Which parts did they like best? Which parts do they think the most important? They could take turns to describe what happened.

Make a collage of a Sikh and/or Christian wedding.

Development

Ask the children what they are responsible for in their lives (e.g. getting up, cleaning teeth, getting ready for school). What responsibilities do other people take for them (e.g. washing clothes, buying and cooking food, keeping them safe)? What are some of the responsibilities of being married (e.g. looking after each other, bringing up children)? Why do some people decide to marry? Do the children think they will get married one day? Why/why not?

Watchpoints

W1 *Christian wedding: bride and groom, white dress symbolising purity, confetti or rice symbolising fertility, flowers symbolising life. Sikh wedding: bride and groom, red or pink clothes for good luck, garlands of flowers, gold jewellery. More information on page 93.*

Learning outcomes

◆ All should be able to describe the main events of Christian and Sikh weddings and some of the associated symbols.
◆ Some may be able to describe a wedding in more detail, and say what promises the bride and groom make to one another. They might be able to give some of the reasons for which people marry.
◆ A few might be able to explain the significance of the symbols associated with Christian and Sikh marriage.

Good and Bad Deeds

Draw a good and bad deed which you have done this year.

My good deed   My bad deed

What good deeds will you try to do next year?

_____

_____

_____

_____

_____

Key concepts	Symbolism, belonging, beliefs and values
Key words	Light, celebrate, suffering, festival
Resources	◆ Poster 4 ◆ PS6 ◆ Materials for greetings cards ◆ Background information (page 94)

Special Times

Wesak

Focus: Buddhism

Background

Wesak commemorates the main events in the life of the Buddha. Buddhists in different parts of the world celebrate Wesak differently. In Sri Lanka they decorate their homes and streets with lanterns; in Thailand they hang up flags, streamers and garlands of flowers, and have candle-lit processions. Many send greetings cards featuring these things. (See page 94.)

Starting points

Discuss Poster 4. How can we tell that the people are celebrating a festival? **W1** Tell them that the people are Buddhists celebrating the festival of Wesak. What other festivals do the children celebrate with lights? **W2** Talk about the feelings of celebration: looking forward to it, the excitement, the wonder.

Activities

Explain that at Wesak Buddhists remember the good and bad things they have done during the past year. The children could complete PS6 about their good and bad deeds.

They could design greetings cards for Wesak. What symbols would they use on the cards (lanterns, garlands, birds flying free)?

Development

Encourage the children to think about significant events in their own lives. **W3** Discuss anything memorable which has happened to the class or school. How could they commemorate this each year, and on what date? Plan a celebration; ask them to consider how to get ready for it, with decorations and a procession.

Tell the children about some of the Buddha's instructions to his followers: they should do all they can to stop people suffering and should always try to have good thoughts. Discuss some of the things which make people suffer. How could we help to stop the suffering of others? **W4**

Watchpoints

W1 *Notice the happy expressions, what people are doing and carrying, the bird being freed, the street decorations.*

W2 *Other festivals of lights include Divali, Christmas and Hanukkah.*

W3 *Special events might include the day they realised they could read, a visit to a special place, or meeting a special person.*

W4 *Suffering might include poverty, sickness, death of loved ones and being hurt by unkind words and deeds. Sometimes we try to help by giving money to charities.*

Learning outcomes

◆ All should be able to describe some ways of celebrating Wesak, and the feelings of people taking part in processions and other Wesak celebrations. They should be able to say why they remember significant events in their own lives.

◆ Some might know that Wesak commemorates the life of the Buddha.

◆ A few might be able to describe some of his teachings: the importance of stopping people's suffering.

The Story of Divali

Write about these characters from the story.

Dasharata _____

Kaikeyi _____

Ravana _____

The Monkey King _____

☆ Who was brave? _____

☆ Who kept his promise? _____

Key concept	Belonging
Key words	Rangoli, good and evil
Resources	◆ Story 'Rama and Sita' (page 80) ◆ PS7
	◆ PS31 ◆ Coloured chalks

Divali

Background

Divali commemorates the legend of Rama and Sita which, like many Hindu stories, shows the struggle between good and evil, where good is the victor (see page 80). It is celebrated during the Hindu months of Aashvin and Kartik (September/October). A diva is a light and Divali means a row of lights, which commemorate the lights lit to welcome Rama and Sita back from exile.

Focus: Hinduism

Starting points

Read the story of Rama and Sita and ask the children to name the characters they think are 'good' and those they think are 'evil'. Does good or evil win in the end?

Talk about other stories where 'good' wins. The children could take turns to re-tell them. Talk about times when good does not win.

Activities

Ask the children to complete the character studies on PS7. They could make masks of the characters in the story (Rama, Sita, Ravana, the Monkey King and the other monkeys). These could be used in acting the story, or as part of a Divali display. The children could use chalk to make the symmetrical rangoli patterns which are placed in doorways (see PS31). Some may be able to make these patterns using art software on a computer.

Discuss the lights used to welcome Rama and Sita back. How must they have felt when they saw all the lights? The children could paint pictures of Rama and Sita's return home.

Development

The children could discuss, draw and write about their own ideas of good and evil. What good things have they seen happening in school, in the community or on television? What have they seen which is evil? They could research such a story to re-tell or write.

They could list some of the good things with which they would like to start a new year. If they could have something blessed for the start of a new year, what would they choose?

Watchpoints

W1 *Rangoli patterns are traditionally made from coloured ground rice. Hindus whose families come from different regions of India celebrate Divali in slightly different ways. Many exchange gifts and cards. Hindu children may associate the goddess Lakshmi with Divali. The celebration of the New Year comes immediately after Divali; Lakshmi is the goddess of good fortune who is believed to visit each home at this time.*

Learning outcomes

◆ All should be able to identify the 'good' characters in the story (Rama, Sita, the monkeys, the Monkey King) and the 'evil' ones (Ravana, Kaikeyi).

◆ Some may be able to explain some of the traditional ways of celebrating Divali: the lamps and the rangoli patterns.

◆ A few might be able to make links between good and evil in the story and their own experiences.

Hanukkah

Label the pictures.

hanukiah	dreidl	Temple
oil		the date of Hanukkah

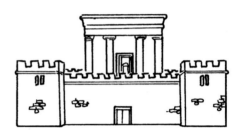

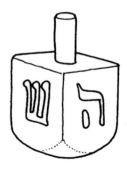

Key concepts	Symbolism, belonging
Key words	Temple, hanukiah, dreidl, celebrate, commemorate
Resources	◆ PS8 ◆ PS32 & 33 ◆ Story 'Judas Maccabaeus and the Temple' (page 82) ◆ Beads, card for spinners ◆ Hanukiah (if possible) ◆ Extra information (page 95)

Hanukkah

Background

Hanukkah begins on 25 Kislev (the third month of the Jewish calendar, which usually corresponds approximately with December) and continues for eight days. It commemorates the defeat of the Syrians by Judas Maccabaeus and his followers, and the cleansing and re-dedication of the temple (see the story on page 82). During the celebrations a hanukiah (which holds nine candles) replaces the menorah (seven-branched candle-holder used on Shabbat).

Focus: Judaism

Starting points

Show the children a picture of a hanukiah (PS32). Read the story on page 82 and ask the children to count the candles on the hanukiah. Why are there eight, plus the one in the middle? Can they explain why Hanukkah lasts for eight days?

Activities

The children could draw a hanukiah, to which they add a new flame each day, beginning with the servant candle and the first candle on the left on the first day.

Show them how to play the traditional Hanukkah dreidl game (see PS33).

Explain that the four letters on the spinner are the initial letters of a Hebrew sentence meaning 'A great miracle happened here'. What was the miracle?

Use PS8 to focus on symbols of Hanukkah. Discuss their meanings in relation to the story.

Development

Help the children to plan and act the story of Judas Maccabaeus. They should decide how many scenes to have and where they should take place, and what the characters would do and say.

Watchpoints

◆ *If possible show a real hanukiah, with the candles burning. They can be obtained from educational suppliers or from a synagogue shop.*

◆ *The central candle is the shammash or servant candle used to light the other eight, which symbolise the eight days the oil lasted in the story. A new candle is lit each day of Hanukkah.*

◆ *Traditionally the game is played with nuts and raisins, not counters.*

Learning outcomes

◆ All should be able to say that Hanukkah is a festival celebrated by Jews to commemorate the saving of the temple, and to re-tell the story. They should be able to describe some of the ways in which Jews celebrate Hanukkah.

◆ Some might be able to say why there are eight main branches on the hanukiah and eight days in Hanukkah.

◆ A few may be able to explain the significance of the Hebrew letters used in the dreidl game.

Coconut Barfi

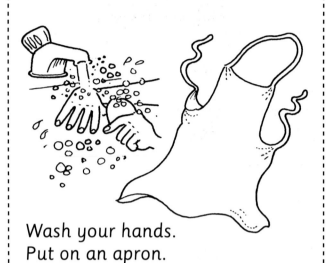

Wash your hands.
Put on an apron.

A grown-up does this.

Heat the milk and sugar.

Stir in the coconut.
The mixture makes a ball.

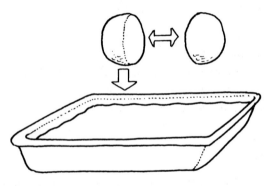

Spread half the mixture in a tray.

Mix red food colouring into the other half.

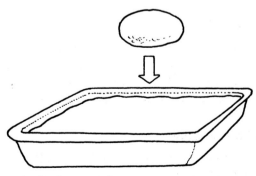

Spread the pink mixture on top of the rest.

Key concepts   Commitment, belonging, lifestyle

Key words   Fast, feast, Ramadan

Resources   PS9 and ingredients   ◆ Calendar of festivals
(page 97)

Id ul-Fitr

Background

Id ul-Fitr is a happy festival which marks the end of Ramadan (when devout Muslims fast during daylight hours and try to put Allah (God) before all else). Id ul-Fitr celebrates the glory of Allah and each individual's achievement of fasting during Ramadan. It begins as soon as the new moon is sighted at the end of Ramadan. Many Muslims go to the mosque for prayers wearing their best clothes and greet one another with the words 'Id Mubarak' (blessed festival). Cards and gifts are exchanged and friends and relatives visit one another.

Focus: Islam

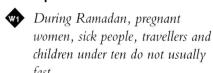

Starting points

Ask the children to think what it must be like to fast. Explain that, for Muslims, fasting shows that they are not thinking of themselves or of everyday things, but of God.

Have the children ever given up anything for a religious reason? They could explain why they did it, how well they managed it and how they felt afterwards. How do they think Muslims feel towards the end of each day of a fast, and as the end of Ramadan approaches? Talk about things to which the children have looked forward, how they felt and how they prepared for these events.

Activities

The children could draw and write about the excitement of Muslims as the new moon at the end of Ramadan is first spotted or when the signal of its arrival is heard from the mosque, or on the radio or television.

Help the children to make coconut barfi, a traditional sweet eaten at Id ul-Fitr, using the recipe on PS9. Afterwards cut up the pictures and ask the children to put them in the correct order.

Development

Ask the children to imagine how fasting might affect their own families. Help them to find the times of sunset and sunrise for Ramadan this year. **W2** At what times could Muslims over the age of ten eat? At what times would they get up and go to bed?

Watchpoints

W1 *During Ramadan, pregnant women, sick people, travellers and children under ten do not usually fast.*

W2 *The dates of all Muslim festivals move forward by eleven days each year because of the Islamic lunar calendar.*

Learning outcomes

◆ All should know that Id ul-Fitr is a Muslim feast after the fast of Ramadan, and that fasting is doing without food. They should be able to describe special events in their lives to which they have looked forward.

◆ Some might be able to explain that fasting during Ramadan helps Muslims to think of Allah (God).

◆ A few might be able to describe the feelings experienced as Muslims wait for the new moon which shows that Ramadan has ended and Id ul-Fitr is beginning.

Advent Calendar

Cut out six pictures to put on
an Advent calendar.

You need
old Christmas cards
and glue.

Stick them on this chart. Label them.

Which is your favourite? ————————————

Why? ————————————————

Key concepts Belonging, beliefs

Key words Advent, nativity, angel, preparation

Resources
- ◆ PS10 ◆ Used Christmas cards
- ◆ Pictures showing angels

Advent

Background

Advent, which means 'coming' (the coming of Jesus), is a time of preparation for Christmas. It begins four Sundays before Christmas.  In churches the reading on the first Sunday is usually the account of the Annunciation (when God sent the angel Gabriel to tell Mary that she was to be the mother of Jesus). An Advent calendar has 24 windows, one of which is opened on each of the 24 days preceding Christmas. Inside each window is a symbol or picture connected with Christmas.

Focus: Christianity

Starting points

Ask the children to think of important events for which they have helped to prepare. What was the first thing which had to be done? What other preparations were needed as the day drew nearer? **W2** Ask the children to take turns to re-tell the story of the Nativity.

Activities

Provide Christmas cards from which the children can cut images of preparation for Christmas (e.g. the Annunciation, Advent wreaths, calendars, candles, cakes, puddings, trees and decorations). They could stick them on PS10. What does each image make them think of?

Make a three-dimensional Advent calendar, using 24 small boxes, all of the same size and shape. Put in each box a Christmas symbol (e.g. Christmas card picture, small decoration, gift from a cracker). The children could write the Christmas story, beginning with the Annunciation, in 24 brief sections and put them in the correct order into the boxes. Each day a child can open a box and display, name and describe its contents; another child can read the story aloud. **W3**

Development

The children could use library books, including children's Bibles, and the words of Christmas carols to find out how different people knew about the coming of Jesus and where to look for him.

They could find out about the role of angels in the Christmas story. What were they like? What did they do? What was special about them? **W4** They could write stories from an angel's point of view.

Watchpoints

W1 *Most Christian denominations celebrate Christmas on 25 December.*

W2 *Responses might include saving up, looking at brochures, booking tickets, choosing and wrapping gifts and keeping them secret, buying new clothes and preparing decorations.*

W3 *On some days more than one box will need to be opened, to compensate for weekends and the school holidays.*

W4 *Christians and Muslims believe angels are messengers of God.*

Learning outcomes

- ◆ All should know that Christians prepare for Christmas in Advent, and be able to describe an Advent calendar and how it is used.
- ◆ Some might be able to explain their choices of contents for the Advent calendar boxes.
- ◆ A few may be able to describe the role of an angel as a messenger from God, and some of the important roles of angels at the time of the Nativity.

infant RE

UNIT 2

Special People

INTRODUCTION

This Unit begins by introducing the idea of people who do things which make them special. Some have special roles, such as community faith leaders, or are people who have a special job within their faith community.

The children learn about the roles of people of the past in founding or developing their religions; the concepts of authority, obedience and being chosen by God are introduced. The children are asked to consider the questions which these people tried to answer. A theme which pervades this Unit is that of the devotion to God of people who were willing to give up worldly things (and sometimes even their lives) in order to help others, to serve God or to be true to their beliefs.

The stories of key figures from Buddhism, Christianity, Islam, Judaism and Sikhism are told, with particular reference to their teaching; the instructions which they gave to their followers; and the ways in which they helped people to understand these instructions.

Unit 2 – Overview

Lesson	Contents	Key Concepts	Religious Focus
1	**Special People in the Community** There are special people in every community: ◆ People who do things which make them special. ◆ What makes some people special? ◆ The concept of leadership.	Belonging	General
2	**Anglican Minister** The role of an Anglican minister: ◆ The special clothing worn by various groups. ◆ How the minister helps parishioners. ◆ The special clothes worn by a minister.	Authority, belonging	Christianity
3	**Jesus the Healer** The emphasis of this lesson is on faith:. ◆ Stories of Jesus healing people who had faith. ◆ Miracles. ◆ What do we think miracles are?	Beliefs, authority, inspiration	Christianity
4	**Jesus the Teacher** The focus is on the stories which Jesus told about what God wanted people to do: ◆ The Sermon on the Mount, including the Beatitudes and the Two Great Commandments. ◆ The Christian ideal of loving one's enemies. ◆ The concept of obedience.	Lifestyle, authority, inspiration	Christianity

Lesson	Contents	Key Concepts	Religious Focus
5	**St Francis of Assissi** The ways in which saints show commitment to their faith: ♦ What do we know about saints? ♦ What does it mean to be a saint? ♦ St Francis of Assisi. ♦ Which things in life are of value? Which are essential and which could be done without?	Beliefs, values, commitment	Christianity
6	**Moses** What it might feel like to be in the presence of God, to be chosen by him for a special job: ♦ What was special about Moses? ♦ The story of the birth of Moses, and of Moses and the Burning Bush. ♦ What is a prophet?	Beliefs and values, authority, inspiration	Judaism
7	**The Mu'adhin** The special role and nature of the mu'adhin: ♦ Familiar everyday sounds, which give people messages. ♦ The adhan (call to prayer) as a special sound. ♦ The story of Bilal: commitment to a religious belief even to the point of being willing to die for it.	Commitment, lifestyle	Islam
8	**Guru Nanak** What a guru is in Sikhism, and the special characteristics of Guru Nanak: ♦ The meaning and benefits of meditation. ♦ A story of a miracle, where someone meets God and is changed by the experience. ♦ Giving up worldly possessions in order to help others. ♦ The use of songs to help people to praise God.	Commitment, authority, inspiration	Sikhism
9	**Guru Gobind Singh** The themes of commitment and making promises: ♦ The militant approach of Guru Gobind Singh, who challenges people to prove their faith. ♦ Making and keeping promises. ♦ Joining and being committed to groups.	Commitment, authority, inspiration	Sikhism
10	**The Buddha** The focus is on someone who was destined to be special: ♦ The story of the Buddha and his enlightenment. ♦ Meditation. ♦ The symbolism of the Buddha's hands. ♦ The concept of suffering and its causes.	Authority, inspiration, lifestyle, beliefs and values	Buddhism

CERTIFICATE

This certificate was awarded to the special person

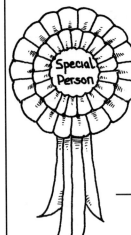

_____

for

_____

_____

_____

_____

Awarded by _____

Key concept Belonging

Key words Commemorate, leader, example, community

Resources ◆ PS11

Special People in the Community

Background

A community can be any group of people with a shared purpose, such as work, education, an interest, shared living space. This lesson is concerned with the local (neighbourhood) community of the children and/or their school.

Focus: General

Starting points

Ask the children to think of someone special in the neighbourhood, and to imagine the person doing the things which make him or her special. Who are these people and what is special about them?

Activities

Ask the children to bring any certificates they have been awarded. What did they have to do to gain them?

PS11 invites the children to design a certificate to award to a special person. Ask them to think about what makes the person special and to write about it and/or draw a picture.

Talk about the ways in which special people are commemorated after they have died (e.g. plaques on houses, names of roads, buildings, schools). Look for such examples in the neighbourhood. **W1**

Ask the children to reflect on 'setting an example'. They could describe times when they have set a good example to younger children. They could prepare a presentation on someone they know, or someone famous, who sets a good example. **W2**

Development

Talk about leaders. Can the children name any leaders? Whom do/did they lead? Ask the children to identify their own leaders. **W3** What do leaders do to make others listen to them, to keep order and to get things done? Talk about the personal qualities of good leaders. **W4**

Watchpoints

W1 *You may need to do some research first, referring to local history or guide books.*

W2 *Distinguish between special people who have become famous as a result of their abilities (e.g. footballers, singers) and those who have served the community in some way, although many of the former could also fall into the latter category.*

W3 *Examples of such leaders include teachers, head teachers and club leaders.*

W4 *It might help if you present these as questions: What might a kind person do? What might a patient person do?*

Learning outcomes

◆ All should be able to identify special people in their local community, and to say what makes them special. They should be able to describe how some special people have been commemorated.

◆ Some might be able to identify the reasons for which some special people are commemorated.

◆ A few might be able to describe some of the things which leaders need to be able to do and what special personal qualities they need.

The Minister's Day

The day of the week

is _____

This is what the minister does.

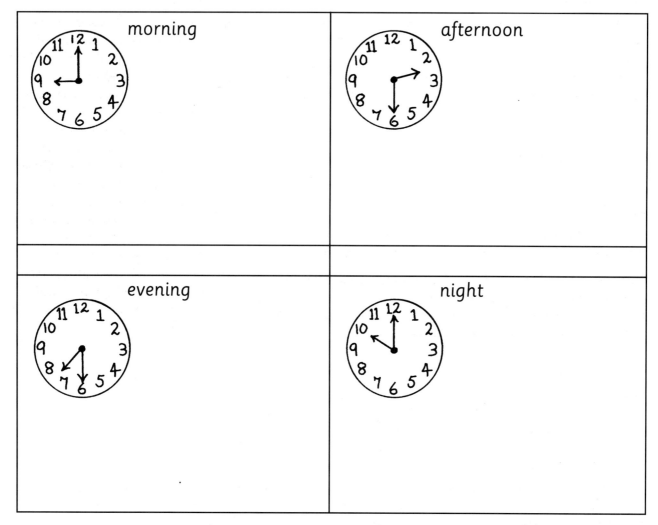

morning

afternoon

evening

night

What else does the minister do?_____

_____

Key concepts Authority, belonging

Key words Leader, vestments, uniform, minister

Resources ◆ Poster 1 ◆ PS12

Anglican Minister

Background

The minister shown in the poster is Anglican. Some denominations of Christianity have male ministers only. Vestments (robes) vary from one denomination to another. Some denominations do not have any robes at all, e.g. Baptists and House Church leaders.

Focus: Christianity

Starting points

If possible visit a church or ask a minister to bring vestments to show to the children. Ask him/her for a copy of his/her typical week's diary. Discuss the minister's special clothes. Can the children name other people who wear special clothes? **W1** Why do they wear them? Who wears a uniform to show people what job they are doing? Why do ministers wear special clothes?

Do the children have any uniforms to show that they belong to a group? You could have a special clothes day when those who have such uniforms can wear them to school. Discuss school uniforms.

Activities

Ask the children to find out about people who wear uniforms for their work, and about symbols, badges or their emblems.

Talk about the minister's diary. What does he or she do apart from leading church services? **W2** Help the children to complete PS12. Ask them to draw the minister at the times shown, and write a sentence below each picture to say what he or she is doing.

Development

Begin a class book about Christian ministers, to which the children can add information, photographs and drawings of items used by ministers and of ministers doing their work.

Watchpoints

W1 *Responses might include: building workers in overalls, steel-capped boots, hard hats; bakers in overalls and hats; police officers in uniforms; motor cyclists in crash helmets and protective clothes.*

W2 *The work of many ministers is similar to that of a social worker, visiting people in need and offering them support; but the minister's work includes spiritual as well as practical help. Most ministers lead meetings of church committees. Many are members of school governing bodies and take an active part in the running of the school and in leading acts of collective worship.*

Learning outcomes

◆ All should be able to describe some of the things a Christian minister does. They should know that the minister is the leader of the church and may wear special clothes to show this.

◆ Some might be able to describe the minister's work in some detail, including types of church service and work with people of the parish.

◆ A few might be able to describe some of the similarities and differences between religious leaders from different denominations of Christianity.

Jesus the Healer

Key concepts Beliefs, authority, inspiration

Key words Miracle, faith

Resources
- ◆ PS13 ◆ Story 'The Woman in the Crowd and Jairus' Daughter' (page 83)
- ◆ Large piece of fabric such as a curtain, scissors, glue

Jesus the Healer

Background

The four gospels in the New Testament of the Bible describe the teaching, healing and miracles of Jesus. Christians interpret some of the stories of healing as the way Jesus showed people the power of God, and the strength which they could have by believing in him and living in the way he wanted them to.

Focus: Christianity

Starting points

Talk about the children's understanding of 'miracles'.

Ask them about events they think are miracles. What makes something a miracle? Introduce the idea of an event which people think cannot happen naturally. Ask the children to describe miracles which they would like to happen.

Activities

Read and discuss the story about Jesus healing people (page 83).

In groups, the children could plan and act short plays based on the story of the woman who touched the hem of Jesus' cloak.

The children could draw Jairus with thought bubbles to show what he was thinking at different points in the story.

Using PS13 the children should cut out the scenes from the story, glue them to a sheet of paper in the correct order and write a sentence below each to tell the story. They should draw the missing last picture (the child getting up).

The children could write and draw their own miracle stories.

Development

Talk about faith. What do the children believe about God? They could draw and write about their faith, or lack of it. What sort of things can they believe without any proof?

Watchpoints

 The children might have heard the word 'miracle' in advertisements: miracle cure, or miracle cleaner. Miracles may seem to the children as 'magic' stories, like fairy tales. Emphasise the importance to Christians of their faith in God and in Jesus.

 Other stories of healing include the man with the withered hand (Matthew 12.9–14, Mark 3.1–6, Luke 6.6–11); the deaf-mute (Mark 7.31–37); the blind man of Bethsaida (Mark 8.22–26); the widow of Nain (Luke 7.11–17); and the bent woman (Luke 13.10–17).

Learning outcomes

- ◆ All should be able to re-tell the story of the woman in the crowd and Jairus's daughter, and to describe something which they think might have been a miracle.
- ◆ Some might know that Jesus is thought by Christians to have been able to heal people by God's power.
- ◆ A few might be able to describe the meaning of faith and to say how they think the woman was cured by touching Jesus' cloak.

Trying to Love Enemies

Key concepts Lifestyle, authority, inspiration

Key words Love, forgive, enemy, teach, authority

Resources ◆ PS14 ◆ Extra information (page 95)

Jesus the Teacher

Background

During the Sermon on the Mount Jesus taught his disciples and others how they should live, and in the Beatitudes he told them about the personal qualities, beliefs and faith which would be rewarded in Heaven (see page 95).

Focus: Christianity

Starting points

Ask the children about things they have learned to do. Who taught them? Of whom would the children ask advice? Why?

Activities

W1 Jesus told his followers to love everyone, even those who treated them badly. What do the children do if others hurt them? How could they obey Jesus? Ask them to complete PS14 by showing the boy's thoughts, and then his words, if he were to obey Jesus.

There is a school in Yorkshire which has only one rule: be considerate. Can the children think of just one or two rules which would ensure that everyone followed all the others? **W2**

Remind the children of the Ten Commandments. **W3** Tell them about the Two Great Commandments of Jesus. **W4** If everyone obeyed these, would they need the Ten Commandments?

Jesus gave examples of the right kind of behaviour. The children could draw and write about examples of this.

Development

Whom do the children obey? Why? Talk about the meaning of 'authority'. The children could draw or find pictures of people with authority. What gives a person authority? What gave Jesus authority, and why did people listen to him? **W5**

Watchpoints

W1 *The activities are appropriate for children of all faith backgrounds or none. Use the words, 'If you were obeying Jesus...', or 'If you were a Christian...'.*

W2 *The rules: 'help others', 'speak kindly to people', and 'move slowly and watch out for other people' could be replaced by 'Think of others'.*

W3 *The story of the Ten Commandments is in Book 1.*

W4 *The Two Great Commandments of Jesus are: Love the Lord your God with all your heart, with all your soul, with all your strength, and with all your mind; and your neighbour as yourself.*

W5 *Jesus is often described, in the Bible, as teaching with authority: people recognised that he spoke with God's authority; they recognised his goodness; his healing and miracles showed them that he was special.*

Learning outcomes

◆ All should be able to describe things they have learned, and to say who taught them. They should identify some of the teachings of Jesus, including 'Love your enemies', and be able to suggest, if not write, the missing thoughts and words for PS14.

◆ Some might be able to identify people with authority and to say what gives them that authority. They might be able to give examples which show what made Jesus special.

◆ A few might be able to explain what makes some people difficult to love and how they could show love to them. They might be able to explain what Jesus would want people to do.

A Saint for Today

Colour the things to give up.

List the things to keep.

How might this woman help others?

Key concepts   Beliefs and values, commitment

Key words   Saint, faith, Heaven

Resources   ◆ PS15   ◆ Story 'St Francis of Assisi'
(page 84) ◆ Other stories about the lives of
saints

Saint Francis of Assisi

Background

The stories of the lives of saints show how they devoted their lives
to serving God by following the teaching of Jesus. Some are
renowned for their visions (e.g. St Bernadette of Lourdes, St Paul).
Others were martyred for refusing to give up their Christian beliefs
(e.g. St Thomas More, St Catherine of Alexandria).

Focus: Christianity

Starting points

Which saints' names do the children know? 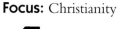 List the responses
and give information about some of the saints named.

What is a saint? Collect the children's ideas; doing so will give an
indication of their level of understanding at the outset.

Activities

Read and discuss the story St Francis of Assisi (page 84). Discuss
the things which Francis had valued before and after he had
changed his way of life. **W2** Help the children to paint portraits of
Francis before and after he changed his lifestyle, showing how he
changed his way of dressing, and including the things he valued.

Use PS15 to help the children to imagine a present-day person
changing in the same way as St Francis did. What sort of lifestyle
might she have? What would she give up to be able to serve God
and to help poor people? They could write their own stories,
showing how a saint could serve God and other people.

Development

Remind the children of the teaching of Jesus and ask them what
St Francis did to obey Jesus.

Talk about the ways in which the children are rewarded for
good behaviour in school, and of times when their own feelings rewarded them, perhaps when they have helped or done
something special for someone. Ask them how saints are
rewarded. **W3**

Watchpoints

W1 *Examples could include patron
saints (St Andrew, St George);
surnames (St John); trade names
(St Michael); place names
(St Helens, St Albans, Bury
St Edmunds); or names of local
churches and schools.*

W2 *He realised that people were worth
more than all his riches, and that
the most important thing to do was
to serve God.*

W3 *During their lifetimes they may be
rewarded by knowing that they are
doing God's will. An important
Christian belief is that people who
live as Jesus taught them will be
rewarded in Heaven.*

Learning outcomes

◆ All should be able to retell the story of St Francis of Assisi, saying what he did to help others.
◆ Some might be able to describe the experiences which made St Francis change his way of life.
◆ A few might be able to describe the lives of other saints, finding similarities and differences between the
ways in which they served God.

The Baby in the Bulrushes

_____

_____

_____

_____

_____

_____

_____

_____

_____

Key concepts   Beliefs and values, authority and inspiration

Key words   Pharaoh, Israelites, slaves

Resources
◆ PS16 Story 'The Birth of Moses' (page 85)
◆ Moses basket (or photograph), if possible

Moses

Background

Focus: Judaism

Moses is a key figure in Christianity and Islam as well as in Judaism; he was the leader of the Jewish people, who took them from slavery in Egypt to the promised land of Canaan. Moses was chosen by God to be the leader of the Israelites. Exodus 12 describes the flight from Egypt, when Moses gave the Israelites God's instructions as to how they should prepare to leave Egypt.

Starting points

Show or describe a Moses basket, used as a baby's cradle. The story is about a baby who had to be hidden in a basket in a river. Why should anyone want to hide a baby boy?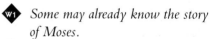

Activities

Tell the story of Moses (page 85). Why did Pharaoh's daughter save him? Talk about the clever plan which Moses' mother had made to save him and to keep him with her without any danger. The children could identify and label the people on PS16. What do they think each one is saying or thinking?

Development

Ask the children to imagine that they are walking along some grassland at the edge of a desert. Talk about the things around them: the sounds, the feel of the hot sun and the hot air in their nostrils, a few dried-up bushes. Suddenly one of the bushes seems to be on fire, but it is not burning away. They go to take a closer look; and then they hear a voice: who is it?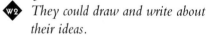

Tell the children that in another story about Moses it was God's voice, saying, 'Come no nearer. Take off your sandals, for this is holy ground. I am the God of your forefathers.' Moses covered his face; he was afraid to look at God. Then God told him he had been watching the Israelites suffering as slaves and that the time had come to help them. Moses must ask Pharaoh to free them. It would not be easy to persuade Pharaoh, but God would help Moses. ◆₃

Ask the children why they think God made the bush burn. Why didn't he just speak to Moses?

Watchpoints

◆₁ *Some may already know the story of Moses.*

◆₂ *They could draw and write about their ideas.*

◆₃ *This could be told to the children as a separate story (see Exodus 3.1–6).*

Learning outcomes

◆ All should be able to re-tell the story of the birth of Moses. They should know that the Israelites were slaves in Egypt and that their baby boys were being killed by the pharaoh.

◆ Some might be able to re-tell the story of the Burning Bush.

◆ A few might know that Moses was chosen by God to be the leader of the Israelites.

The Mu'adhin

Finish the sentences.

Choose words from the box.

Allah	**Muhammad**	**loud**
clear	**healthy**	
five	**prayer**	

The mu'adhin must be _____.

He has to know the _____ times.

He has to have a _____,
_____ voice.

He calls Muslims to prayer _____
times a day.

He praises _____ and says that
He is the only God.

He says that Allah's messenger is
_____ (pbuh).

Key concepts Commitment, lifestyle

Key words Muslim, prayer, adhan, minaret, responsibility

Resources ◆ Poster 5 ◆ PS17 ◆ The story of 'Bilal' (page 85) ◆ The call to prayer (page 96) ◆ A recording of the call to prayer, if possible ◆ A tape recorder

The Mu'adhin

Background

The mu'adhin calls Muslims to prayer five times a day. He (mu'adhins are always male) must be sound in body and mind and know the times of prayer for each day. He needs a strong, clear voice since he goes to the top of the minaret (mosque tower) five times a day, faces the qibla (the direction of Makkah), cups his hands and calls out the words which have remained unchanged since 622 CE, during the time of Muhammad (pbuh).

Focus: Islam

Starting points

Talk about sounds which give us messages ◆. What do they tell us to do? What other sounds tell us to stop what we are doing and do something else?

If possible, play a recording of the call to prayer and explain that it tells people to stop what they are doing, ready to do something else. Tell them that it is the adhan, calling Muslims to prayer. ◆

Explain that the man shown on Poster 5 calls the adhan. What do they notice about the place from which he calls?

Activities

Display pictures of things whose sounds tell people to stop one action and do another.

Read and discuss the story of Bilal (page 85).

Ask the children to complete PS17, showing the sort of person the mu'adhin has to be and what he has to know and be able to do.

If the children could shout a special message from the top of a tall tower, what would it be? They could try it. Tape-record them. How did they feel after shouting their messages?

Development

The children could write a daily diary of a mu'adhin. How might he feel going up the great tower and when he calls out the important words? What characteristics does he need?

Watchpoints

W1 *When Muslims mention a prophet's name they always say 'Peace be upon him'. In written English this is abbreviated to 'pbuh'.*

W2 *Such sounds include: telephone ringing; doorbell; fire alarm; car horn; school bell.*

W3 *Muslims pray five times a day wherever they are. They need not go to the mosque; most of their prayers, particularly for women and children, take place at home. The adhan praises God, states the Muslim belief that Allah is the only God and that Muhammad (pbuh) is his messenger; then it calls people to pray, and ends by praising God.*

Learning outcomes

◆ All should be able to describe the main task of the mu'adhin and know that the call is made from a minaret, part of a mosque, which is where Muslims worship.

◆ Some might be able to repeat some of the words of the adhan and know that it is very important to Muslims. They might be able to think of an important message of their own.

◆ A few may be able to write about the mu'adhin's day, describing the characteristics he needs.

Guru Nanak

Which words describe Guru Nanak?

Colour the boxes.

noisy	calm

peaceful	warlike	quiet

mean	kind	holy

What is Guru Nanak doing?

Circle the words.

singing   thinking   praying

talking   sitting   kneeling

Finish the sentence.

Guru Nanak was special because ————————————

————————————————————————

————————————————————————

————————————————————————

Key concepts	Commitment, authority, inspiration
Key words	Guru, meditate, holy, joyful, peaceful, preaching, devotion
Resources	◆ Poster 6 ◆ PS18 ◆ Guru Nanak's Song (page 87) ◆ Story 'Guru Nanak' (page 87)

Guru Nanak

Background

Guru Nanak (1469–1539 CE), the first of the ten Sikh gurus, was born in the area which is now Pakistan. He was always interested in religion, and by the age of 30 was meditating and composing hymns and psalms, many of which form parts of the Guru Granth Sahib, the Sikh holy book. His joyful yet quiet and peaceful way of worshipping attracted many followers, called Sikhs. **W1**

Focus: Sikhism

Starting points

Show Poster 6. What is the man doing? Discuss the meaning of 'meditate'. **W2** Have the children ever tried to concentrate, but found their minds wandering?

The picture is of Guru Nanak. How can we tell he is special? Point out the glow around his head. What might it mean? Where have the children seen light as a religious symbol? **W3**

Ask the children to think of words which describe Guru Nanak. They might complete PS18.

Activities

Read and discuss the story of Guru Nanak (page 87).

The children could think about the place to which the guru travelled. Help them to imagine themselves doing the same. **W4**

Ask them to imagine this place: what they see, the colours, the smells, the feel of the ground beneath them. Ask them to paint or draw the beautiful place. They could write about their ideas and read their descriptions aloud.

Development

Talk about things which are made easier to learn by singing, such as counting rhymes, rhymes teaching direction and position, songs giving information and instructions.

The children could describe how Guru Nanak's songs might have helped him to teach people about God.

Watchpoints

W1 *Guru means 'teacher'; Sikh means 'disciple'.*

W2 *Explain that 'meditate' means to think calmly and quietly about something, without letting anything else get in the way of these thoughts.*

W3 *Light usually represents God or knowledge of God. In Christian art haloes symbolise holiness.*

W4 *They could begin by sitting quietly, closing their eyes, and picturing themselves somewhere peaceful by a river. Ask them to imagine themselves moving through or across the water, the feel of the water on their bodies, and moving through/across it until they arrive at a beautiful place.*

Learning outcomes

◆ All should be able to describe what makes Guru Nanak look special or holy. They should be able to re-tell the story of Guru Nanak, saying what showed that he had been with God.

◆ Some might be able to re-tell the story in detail, and describe how Guru Nanak used songs to help people to learn about and worship God.

◆ A few may be able to talk about the experiences of people from other faiths with whom God communicated, such as Muhammad (pbuh), Jesus and Moses.

The Khalsa

Key concepts   Commitment, authority, inspiration, lifestyle

Key words   Guru, brave, amrit, faith, promise, volunteer

Resources   ◆ PS19   ◆ Story 'The First Baisakhi' (page 88)

Guru Gobind Singh

Background

Guru Gobind Singh (1666–1708), the tenth guru, established the Khalsa at Baisakhi in 1699. He declared himself the last human guru; the holy book, the Guru Granth Sahib, would become the living guru.

At 13 or 14 many Sikhs take part in a ceremony at which they drink amrit as a symbol of commitment to their faith. **W1** They promise to follow Guru Gobind Singh's rules and to wear the Five Ks.

Focus: Sikhism

Starting points

Have the children ever been asked to volunteer for something? If someone volunteered for an unpleasant or difficult task, what did the children think of him/her?

Read the story on page 88. Ask how the crowd must have felt when the guru asked for someone to die for his faith. **W2**

The Khalsa is a group of people who have promised to obey the rules of Sikhism. Do the children know any of these rules? **W3** What symbols do Sikhs carry to show their faith? On PS19 the children can colour four of the Five Ks. **W4**

The children could think of promises which they and their teacher could make. They could be prioritised to form the basis of a contract.

Activities

The children could describe groups they have joined. Did they make promises? Were they difficult to keep?

Development

The children could compare the rules of Sikhism with those of other religions. **W5** Why do religions have rules?

They could compare the ways in which Guru Nanak and Guru Gobind Singh persuaded people to worship God.

Watchpoints

W1 *Amrit is made from sugar and water.*

W2 *People who were prepared to die for their faith, include Bilal (Islam), Christian martyrs and Jesus.*

W3 *To give money to the gurdwara; to rise early, and wash thoroughly before praying; to say evening and late night prayers; to say the Ardas (formal prayer offered at all Sikh religious services) regularly; to wear the Five Ks and use the name Singh or Kaur; not to cut their hair or eat meat slaughtered by Jewish or Islamic methods; not to smoke, drink or commit adultery.*

W4 *Kirpan (dagger), Kara (bracelet), Kesh (long hair), Khanga (comb). Kachera (shorts) not shown to avoid offence to Sikhs.*

W5 *See Book 1, Unit 3, Lesson 8 and Book 2, Unit 2, Lesson 4*

Learning outcomes

◆ All should be able to describe what Guru Gobind Singh asked his followers to do, name some of the promises he asked them to make and describe promises they themselves have made.

◆ Some might be able to describe in some detail the rules which Guru Gobind Singh laid down for Sikhs and how Sikhs nowadays show that they will obey these rules.

◆ A few might be able to describe the similarities and differences between the rules of different faiths.

Hand signs

Match the hand signs to the words.

| I don't know |
| Hello |
| Come here |
| Don't do that again |
| Good luck |
| That way |
| Well done |
| Me? |

Draw some hand signs.

| I can't hear you. | Look up there! | Goodbye. |

Key concepts	Authority, inspiration, lifestyle, beliefs and values
Key words	Meditate, symbol, enlightenment, holiness
Resources	◆ Poster 7 ◆ PS20 ◆ PS34 ◆ Story 'The Story of Prince Siddhartha Gautama' (page 89)

The Buddha

Background

The Buddha means 'the enlightened one'. The Buddhist scriptures (Dharmapada) describe the feelings of the Buddha (Siddhartha Gautama) during his enlightenment, while he was meditating beneath a bodhi tree. Buddhists revere the Buddha as the man who shared his enlightenment with others; they do not worship him. He lived in northern India (563–483 BCE). Buddhists call their faith the Dharma (teachings of the Buddha).

Focus: Buddhism

Starting points

Ask the children to describe the Buddha (Poster 7), particularly the shape of his head, the position in which he is seated, his clothing, his face (particularly the eyes) and his hands. **W1** Take time to look quietly at the Buddha. What is he doing? How can they tell? What feelings are suggested by the statue? **W2**

Activities

Draw attention to the Buddha's hands; do they seem to be giving any signal? What do they seem to say? **W3** Talk about the ways people can communicate with their hands and ask the children to try. Can the others tell what they mean? Use PS20.

Try a simple form of meditation. Each child needs a flower to look at and to focus on. Ask them to sit crosslegged on the floor with their backs straight and to stretch towards the ceiling as if an invisible thread were pulling the tops of their heads. They should concentrate only on the flower. Do this for about 5–10 minutes, depending on the children's concentration; then ask them to begin to look around the room. Show them how to stretch their arms up to the ceiling as they take a deep breath. How do they feel? Can they explain why the Buddha sat still and meditated?

Development

Read and discuss the story on page 89. Talk about the Buddha's enlightenment. He thought about the meaning of life: why are we here on Earth? Tell the children that nobody really knows the answer to this question and ask them to think about it.

Watchpoints

W1 *Buddhists often have in their homes pictures or statues of the Buddha which they treat with great reverence: they keep them in high places; clean them on festival days; and sometimes sprinkle them with perfumed water.*

W2 *They might think he is praying, meditating or thinking. Feelings might include calm, quietness, peace, stillness, rest, reverence, holiness.*

W3 *The hands of the Buddha show a range of symbolic gestures in different pictures and statues – see PS34. On the poster his hands are in the 'Earth touching' position: asking the Earth to witness his enlightenment.*

Learning outcomes

◆ All should be able to describe the statue of the Buddha and some of the feelings it suggests. They should be able to demonstrate hand signals and explain their meaning.
◆ Some might be able to meditate and describe their feelings afterwards.
◆ A few may be able to express their thoughts about the meaning of life.

Special Places

INTRODUCTION

This Unit introduces the idea of special places by presenting a place which is not linked to any of the major religions, yet is thought to have some religious significance. The children's appreciation of the spiritual is developed during the discussion of a spectacular and awe-inspiring place and the people who might have built it. Ultimate questions are raised before the children consider places which are special because of their shared ownership: the sense of responsibility and belonging to a community is explored.

The Unit proceeds to discuss the idea of the places where people choose to go to be alone with God or to pray and then looks at places of worship, their symbolism and the ways in which they are used. Artefacts used during worship are discussed, and the idea of worshipping at home as well as in a special building. The feelings expressed in the creation of religious buildings are discussed and the children find out about a range of places of worship, before thinking about special journeys and looking at places of pilgrimage, why people go to them and their feelings when they get there.

Unit 3 – Overview

Lesson	Contents	Key Concepts	Religious Focus
1	**A Stone Circle** This lesson focuses on the thoughts and feelings which a picture of a spectacular place inspires: ◆ Why was it built? ◆ How it was used? ◆ What makes a place mysterious?	Belonging, ultimate questions	General
2	**Special Places in the Community** The focus is the consideration which people in a community need to show to one another: ◆ The classroom. ◆ Other shared areas: living space, club and leisure rooms and bedrooms. ◆ Places of worship as community centres.	Belonging	General
3	**A Place for Prayer** The focus is on the purposes and formats of prayers and on being in the presence of God: ◆ The Garden of Gethsemane. ◆ The places which people choose for prayer. ◆ A special place for prayer in the classroom.	Beliefs, ultimate questions	Christianity, Hinduism, Judaism, Sikhism

Lesson	Contents	Key Concepts	Religious Focus
4	**Worshipping at Home** Worship at home is common to many faiths: ◆ The artefacts which Christians and Hindus have in their homes to remind them of their faith. ◆ The idea of ending everyday activities and doing something special when worship is about to begin. ◆ The items on the puja tray.	Symbolism, lifestyle, beliefs	Christianity/ Hinduism
5	**Cathedral** The emphasis in this lesson is on the grandeur of the cathedral: ◆ Its immense and awe-inspiring size. ◆ How the design of the building and the artefacts in it help Christians to worship.	Symbolism, beliefs	Christianity
6	**Synagogue** This lesson focuses on the symbols in the synagogue: ◆ How they are linked to Jewish history. ◆ Moses and the Ten Commandments (Book 1, Unit 3, Lesson 8). ◆ Moses (Unit 2 of this book, Lesson 6).	Symbolism, beliefs	Judaism
7	**Doorways** This lesson emphasises the importance of preparation for prayer: ◆ The transition from one activity to another. ◆ The difficulties sometimes encountered in this. ◆ The significance of a doorway in separating everyday life from reflection, prayer and devotion.	Symbolism, daily life, beliefs	Hinduism
8	**Journeys to Special Places** This lesson explores the planning of and preparing for a journey to a special place: ◆ The children's own special places. ◆ The purpose of the journey. ◆ Places which the children would like to visit.	Belonging	General
9	**Lourdes** This lesson focuses on places where special things have happened: ◆ The sense of belonging which people feel when they travel in groups for a shared purpose. ◆ The story of St Bernadette. ◆ The significance of the shrine at Lourdes.	Belonging, devotion, inspiration	Christianity
10	**Special Places for Buddhists** The four main sites of Buddhist pilgrimage: ◆ The significance of each as the site of an important event in the life of the Buddha. ◆ The idea of developing understanding and insight by visiting these places. ◆ The idea of enlightenment and rebirth. ◆ Some difficult questions.	Beliefs, ultimate questions	Buddhism

The Special Stones

Key concepts Belonging, ultimate questions

Key words Mystery, structure, monument, wonder

Resources ◆ Poster 8 ◆ PS21

A Stone Circle

Background

Focus: General

Calanais, on the Isle of Lewis, is a late Neolithic circle of standing stones surrounding a monolith more than 4m high, and a tiny chambered burial cairn which was in use for at least 800 years. Radiating from this central circle are four arms of stones, one of them forming a double avenue of standing stones.

Starting points

Ask the children to describe what they see in Poster 8. Does it look natural, or as if it was made by people? Is it old or modern? How can they tell? Why did people build this place? What for? Consider how the big stones were moved. Why would people have worked so hard to build the circle? **W1** How is the place special? **W2**

The children could look for similarities between this and other, more modern places, of which they know the purpose.

They could describe special places, made by people long ago, which they have visited or seen in pictures or on television. What was special about them? Were they big or small? How did they make the children feel and what do they remember best about them?

Activities

The children could make models, paint pictures and write descriptions of the stone circle.

Ask the children to imagine they can step into the poster, into the stone circle. What would it feel like to be in this mysterious place? What can they imagine people doing there? They could draw and describe these people and their actions. PS21 helps to focus their thoughts.

Collect pictures of other standing stones for comparison. Why have people made big stone structures? **W3**

Development

Ask the children about places which they find mysterious. **W4**
They could collect pictures of mysterious places.

Watchpoints

W1 *Nobody is sure of the precise purpose of the Calanais monument, but it probably had ritual and religious significance. It took huge labour and remarkable engineering skill to erect the stones, and the community which built it, and looked after it for nearly a millennium, can never have been very large.*

W2 *Some special things are the huge size of the stones, their shapes, their arrangement and their age (c4000 years).*

W3 *Other standing stones include Stonehenge, Easter Island statues, the standing stone at Capel Coch on Anglesey, and the stone circle near Mold in North Wales.*

W4 *Responses might include endless caves and tunnels, bottomless pits and holes, high mountains, huge structures and places of great beauty.*

Learning outcomes

◆ All should understand the huge effort made by ancient peoples to build such structures, and appreciate the mystery of the Calanais stones.

◆ Some might be able to identify other structures which evoke a similar feeling of mystery, and describe the feelings of the people who used them.

◆ A few may be able to identify what it is that makes some places feel mysterious.

Our Classroom

 Good points | Bad points

How I can make our classroom better:

_____

_____

_____

_____

_____

Key concept   Belonging

Key words   Responsibility, co-operation, consideration, community

Resources   ◆ PS22

In the Community

Background

Focus: General

Places used by a community have a purpose; the community has a responsibility to care for, as well as to benefit from, them. Community members who share the planning, creation and care of a special place have a sense of ownership of it. ◆W1◆

Starting points

Ask the children to think about their classroom. To whom does it belong? Who is in charge of it? Who should look after it? Why, and how? What can be done to make it a good place to work in? ◆W2◆

Ask about other rooms the children share. ◆W3◆ With whom do they share, why, and how do they share responsibility for looking after the rooms? How can they show consideration for others when using these rooms?

Activities

Using PS22 in pairs or groups, the children could first identify the good points about the classroom, then look for ways to make it better. With them, decide which suggestions could be put into practice. The children could make before and after pictures or photographs. How have their efforts helped the class community?

The children could draw and write about how they and their families can show consideration in shared rooms.

Development

A small area of the classroom can be turned into a special place with a purpose. Groups of children could plan this special place and share their ideas so that the class can decide which is the best use. ◆W4◆ The whole class could contribute in different ways and over time add ideas to enhance it and keep it special. Ask them to write rules for the use of the special place. ◆W5◆

Watchpoints

◆W1◆ *A community is a group of people who share any or all of the following: beliefs; living, leisure or working accommodation; interests; nationality. Places of worship are often used as community centres.*

◆W2◆ *Consider tidiness, consideration for other people and property, safety, ease of use.*

◆W3◆ *Examples might include: bedrooms, club meeting places, living space, cloakrooms, bathrooms, places of worship.*

◆W4◆ *They should consider its purpose, how they will make and keep it special, when they will use it.*

◆W5◆ *Rules might include the number of people allowed in it, what behaviour is/is not allowed, for how long they can use it.*

Learning outcomes

◆ All should be able to identify some ways in which their classroom is a good place in which to work, some in which it is not, and some possible improvements. They should be able to describe some ways in which they should/should not behave in shared rooms at home.

◆ Some might be able to identify aspects of sharing working space which contribute to a feeling of community, and to describe this feeling.

◆ A few might be able to generate an idea for a special place which the others find convincing, giving a clear picture and instructions as to how the special place can be created.

This is what My Prayer Would Be.

Key concepts Beliefs, ultimate questions

Key words Peace, calm, prayer

Resources ◆ Poster 9 ◆ PS23 ◆ Prayers (page 78)
◆ Magazines, travel brochures, postcards of places

A Place for Prayer

Background

Key religious people went to special places to be in God's presence. The Buddha sat beneath a bodhi tree; Jesus went into the wilderness, and to the Garden of Gethsemane; Guru Nanak sat by a river; Moses went up Mount Sinai; and Muhammad (pbuh) went to a cave on Mount Hjira.

Focus: General

Starting points

Ask the children what sort of place Poster 9 shows. What might they do there? 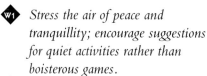 It is the Garden of Gethsemane in Israel, where Jesus used to pray. Why did he go there to be close to God?

Have the children been to peaceful places? How did they feel? They could draw these places to make a 'peaceful places' book.

Do the children ever want to be alone? Why? Where do they go? What do they do there? How does this help them?

Activities

Ask the children to find pictures of places to be alone to pray or to think about God. Why did they choose them?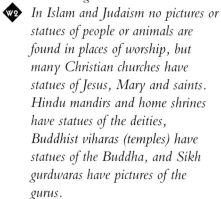

What are prayers for? To whom do people speak when they are praying? **W3** Can people pray without speaking?

Read prayers from different faiths (page 78) and discuss their purposes, e.g. praise, thanks, forgiveness, or to ask God to care for people.

Development

Ask the children to imagine themselves in places to be close to God. What might they say to God? They could discuss their ideas in pairs and draft a prayer, using PS23.

Watchpoints

W1 *Stress the air of peace and tranquillity; encourage suggestions for quiet activities rather than boisterous games.*

W2 *In Islam and Judaism no pictures or statues of people or animals are found in places of worship, but many Christian churches have statues of Jesus, Mary and saints. Hindu mandirs and home shrines have statues of the deities, Buddhist viharas (temples) have statues of the Buddha, and Sikh gurdwaras have pictures of the gurus.*

W3 *Encourage the children to listen to and accept others' ideas. Jews and Muslims address their prayers only to God. Christian prayers may be addressed to God or to Jesus. Hindus worship one god, Brahman, in the form of various deities; Krishna, Shiva, Vishnu and Brahma.*

Learning outcomes

◆ All should recognise the peacefulness of the Garden of Gethsemane and be able to select other pictures with a similar air. They should know that Jesus often went there to pray. They should recognise a few words used in prayers.

◆ Some might be able to describe the feelings of a religious person in a place of prayer. They might be able to describe what people say during prayer, its purposes and to whom they might talk. They might be able to write their own prayers, with help.

◆ A few might be able to describe how people feel when they are close to God. They might be able to compose their own prayers, unaided.

Puja

Match the pictures.

incense

spoon

bell

water pot

kum kum powder

arti lamp

Which senses? ✔

	see 👁	hear 👂	feel ✋	smell 👃	taste 👄
incense					
water					
kum kum					
arti lamp					
bell					
spoon					

Key concepts Symbolism, lifestyle, beliefs

Key words Sign, prayer, devotion, puja

Resources ◆ PS24 ◆ 'Puja' information (page 96)
◆ Artefacts used during worship at home in
Christianity (holy water stoop, crucifix,
pictures of Jesus) ◆ Artefacts used during
worship at home in Hinduism (puja tray)

Worshipping at Home

Background

People from many faiths worship at home. Some Christians pray at
home with objects to help them worship. Other Christians pray
unaided. Most Hindu families have a shrine which might comprise
murtis (pictures or statues of deities), a puja tray (see page 96), and
offerings to the deities. **W1** Offerings are important in Hinduism;
they signify devotion: 'If anyone gives me with devotion a leaf, a
flower, fruit or water, I accept that gift devotedly given from the
giver who gives himself.' (Bhagavad Gita, 9.26)

Focus: Christianity, Hinduism

Starting points

Talk about religious artefacts in homes and cars. **W2** If possible
show artefacts which Christians may have at home. **W3**

Discuss rituals in the children's lives, which may or may not have a
religious connection, and may be part of preparations for a regular
event, such as going to bed, having a meal or visiting relations.

If possible, provide a puja set (see page 96) and let small groups of
children examine it. Ask them what they think Hindus might do
with the items when they worship God. **W4** Talk about ways to
make special a place used for worship, and ask them what they
would see, hear and smell during puja.

Activities

The children could draw or paint a Christian artefact, and write
about the ways in which Christians use it.

PS24 helps the children to identify the main items of the puja
set, and to link them to the senses. How might the artefacts
help Hindus to prepare for worship if they have been busy?

Development

A group could redesign the role-play corner as a Christian or
Hindu home. They should list the things they will need and draw
some of the changes they will make. Discuss with the whole class
the best way to change the role-play corner.

Watchpoints

W1 *Puja is the Hindu act of worship,
which is practised both in temples
and at home. In a Hindu family
the mother or grandmother usually
leads the daily act of worship.*

W2 *Cars and houses might contain
St Christopher medallions, crosses
and crucifixes, stickers with
quotations from the Qur'an or
Bible.*

W3 *A Christian could be invited to
talk to the class, showing how they
use artefacts such as crucifixes and
rosaries to prepare for and during
prayer. Present this as a
demonstration, not an act of
worship, to avoid compromising the
children's own beliefs.*

W4 *A Hindu could be invited to talk to
the class, to show how the artefacts
are used. Take care not to
compromise children's beliefs.*

Learning outcomes

◆ All should be able to name some artefacts which Christians and Hindus have in their homes to remind
them of their faith or to assist their worship, and be able to describe how some of these are used.

◆ Some could explain the symbolism of Hindu artefacts and say to which senses they appeal.

◆ A few might be able to describe the need to stop everyday things to prepare for worship.

Cathedral

Match the pictures.

Key concepts Symbolism, beliefs	UNIT 3
Key words Nave, altar, pew, hassock, hymn board, God	**Special Places**
Resources ◆ Poster 10 ◆ PS25 ◆ Pictures of different churches and cathedrals	LESSON 5

Cathedral

Background

An Anglican or Roman Catholic cathedral is a church which has a bishop (or archbishop) in charge of all the other churches in the diocese. Most cathedrals contain beautiful works of art. Liverpool Anglican Cathedral was designed by Sir Giles Gilbert Scott. It is the second largest cathedral in the world (St Peter's in Rome is bigger). Its distinguishing feature is its size. Its decoration is mainly in stone and wood carving.

Focus: Christianity

Starting points

What do the children notice about the cathedral on Poster 10? Why is it so big? What did the people who had it built want to say about God? **W1** Point out the high altar. What is it for? **W2**

Invite the children to compare the wood and stone carvings with wooden furniture in school and stonework on any buildings they know. What are the differences?

Activities

Ask the children to think of buildings they have visited. How did they feel? How would they feel if they stood in the nave (the long central part) of the cathedral and looked up into the massive tower? They could draw and write about this.

Talk about the artefacts in a church or cathedral; use PS25 to explain their uses. **W3** You could take the children to a cathedral or church, or invite a Christian visitor to talk to them about it.

Development

Collect pictures of churches and cathedrals. What similarities do the children notice? They may see that many have a high spire or tower. Why? They may link this with the idea of God being in 'heaven above'.

Watchpoints

W1 *Point out the relative size of the chairs, which indicates the immensity of the building. A cathedral is usually much larger than an ordinary church. To Christians its size makes it a monument to the greatness of God.*

W2 *The high altar is the holiest part of any cathedral or church. People worshipping in cathedrals and churches do not touch the altar; they go no closer than the rails, which are usually a few metres in front of it.*

W3 *Pews for people to sit on; hymn board to show which hymns to sing; hymn book; hassocks or kneelers to kneel on when praying; lectern to rest a big Bible on; font to hold the water for baptisms.*

Learning outcomes

◆ All should know that a cathedral is a special place of worship for Christians. They should be able to describe some other very large buildings and say how they would feel in them. They should be able to identify some useful features of churches and cathedrals and to describe how they are used.

◆ Some might be able to describe what makes a cathedral special, e.g. size, artwork, and that it has a bishop or archbishop.

◆ A few might be able to link the size and scale of the building with the Christian idea of the greatness of God and 'reaching up to heaven'.

The Synagogue

Which of these can you find on the poster? Tick the boxes. ☑

Match the words to the pictures.

☐

| prayer shawl |

| candle holder |

| everlasting light |

☐

| The Ark |

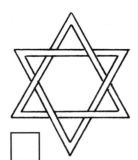

☐

| platform |

| Star of David |

☐

☐

☐

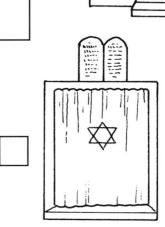

What else can you see in a synagogue? ——————

————————————————————————

————————————————————————

Key concepts	Symbolism, beliefs
Key words	Synagogue, Israelites, symbol, tabernacle, ner tamid, Magen David, menorah
Resources	◆ Poster 11 ◆ PS26

Synagogue

Background

The design of a synagogue is based on the instructions for constructing the Tabernacle which God gave to Moses. 'Synagogue' comes from a Greek word meaning meeting place. **W1** Synagogues can be venues for history, language and scripture classes; children's clubs; a place to buy Jewish artefacts, and for musical or dramatic performances, as well as being places of communal worship.

Focus: Judaism

Starting points

Remind the children about Moses and the Israelites in Egypt (see Unit 2, Lesson 6). When the Israelites escaped from Egypt, Moses led them across the desert to the 'promised land' of Canaan. While they were travelling the Israelites needed a special place to keep the stone tablets on which the Ten Commandments had been written (see Book 1, Unit 3, Lesson 8). God told Moses how to build a 'tabernacle' which they could set up wherever they camped.

Draw attention to the six-pointed Star or Shield of David (Magen David) on the cover of this book. Explain that it is a symbol of Judaism. Have the children seen this symbol elsewhere? **W2** Do the children know any other signs which are symbols of religions?

Activities

The synagogue on Poster 11 is where Jews meet and worship. Can the children find anything in it which reminds them of the stories they know about the Israelites? Use PS26 to focus on the main features. They might notice the plaques bearing the Ten Commandments, the everlasting light, and the lack of statues or pictures of people and animals. **W3** What do they notice about the stained glass?

Development

Talk about the everlasting light (ner tamid) of the Tabernacle; ask the children why God might have wanted it to have this. **W4**

Watchpoints

W1 *Most Jews call the synagogue 'shul'. It is usual for men and women to keep their heads covered in a synagogue; men wear small round caps (kippot, singular kippah) and women wear hats.*

W2 *It may be found in or on synagogues; on other buildings associated with Judaism (kosher butchers' shops, delicatessens, bakeries and restaurants); on the flag of Israel; and on jewellery.*

W3 *No images of people or animals are found in a synagogue since these could be regarded as idols, which are strictly forbidden in Judaism.*

W4 *An important rule which God gave to Moses was that the tabernacle should have a lamp burning at all times, to show that God was there. Nowadays many synagogues use electricity, rather than the traditional oil, for the lamp. The other symbolic light is the menorah (candle holder).*

Learning outcomes

◆ All should know that a synagogue is a Jewish place of worship, and that all synagogues have a special light which is never allowed to go out. They should recognise the Star of David.
◆ Some might be able to describe other features of a synagogue.
◆ A few may be able to explain the meaning of the everlasting light and other features of a synagogue.

A Hindu Temple Doorway

Key concepts Symbolism, daily life, beliefs

Key words Temple, mandir, deity, murti

Resources ◆ Poster 12 ◆ PS27 ◆ Story 'Ganesha' (page 90)

Doorways

Background

The entrances of many Hindu temples (mandirs) in India are decorated with figures of deities, scripture scenes and Hindu symbols (page 90). (W1) Hindus can worship in a temple at any time. They remove their shoes when they enter, wash, and walk around the inside in a clockwise direction. They ring a bell when they enter the shrine room, to alert the deity; they make offerings (milk, flowers, fruit). Before praying the worshipper or priest lights an arti lamp. (W2) Each morning the priest washes and dresses the murtis (statues) in their elaborate costumes. At night he removes the costumes and washes them again. He offers the murtis food and water or milk three times a day.

Focus: Hinduism

Starting points

Begin after playtime and notice how the children enter the classroom. It takes a while to become quiet and ready for work. Can they think of a better way to come into the classroom? Try some of their ideas. (W3)

Show poster 12 and discuss what people might be doing outside the doors, and how their activities change after they have gone inside.

Activities

Use PS27 to discuss the elaborate doorway to a Hindu temple. What can they see on it? How might people feel as they go from everyday activities through the doorway and into the temple?

The children could decorate the classroom door so that as they go through they can prepare their minds for work. What symbols and pictures might they use?

Development

Tell the children about the ways in which Hindus prepare for worship in the temple. How could the children prepare themselves for assembly, so that it becomes a special activity? (W4) Read the story of Ganesha, a Hindu deity who is often represented in mandirs (page 90).

Watchpoints

(W1) *Many Hindu temples in Britain are converted buildings.*

(W2) *Arti is a welcoming ceremony to prepare people for worship.*

(W3) *They might stand still for a while, walk slowly round the building, take deep breaths.*

(W4) *The children could design and make a special doorway decoration for the school hall.*

Learning outcomes

◆ All should be able to describe how feelings change at the end of one activity and the start of another, and how to prepare themselves for special activities. They should know that the mandir is a temple where Hindus worship.

◆ Some may be able to explain how the temple doorway helps Hindus to focus on worship.

◆ A few might understand the significance of symbolic preparations for worship.

A Special Journey

I am going to:

I shall take:

I shall sing:

I shall tell this story:

I shall play:

I shall think about:

Key concept: Belonging

Key word Pilgrimage

Resources ◆ PS28 ◆ Poem 'The End of the Road' (page 79)

Journeys to Special Places

Focus: General

Background

Most religions have places of pilgrimage: Varanasi, India (the Buddha's first sermon – Buddhism); Lourdes, France (the visions of St Bernadette – Christianity); the source of Ganga, India (source of a sacred river – Hinduism); Makkah, Saudi Arabia (the holiest building, the Kabah – Islam); Jerusalem, Israel (the West Wall, all that remains of the Temple – Judaism); Amritsar, India (the site of the Golden Temple – Sikhism).

Starting points

Ask the children to think of a place where they have never been, and which they would very much like to visit. Why do they want to go there? What is special about the place? How might they be able to go there one day? They could draw and write about it.

Activities

Talk about the feeling of belonging to a group. What do some people in groups do to show that they are all travelling for the same purpose?

The children could plan special journeys in pairs. Where will they go? What do they need to take? What will they do during the journey? They could design something to wear to show the purpose of the journey.

Read the poem on page 79, then ask the children to name some of the words which the poet used to describe the ways in which he moved during the journey. They could mime some of the actions, and make up their own mime of a long journey.

Development

If possible invite someone who has made a pilgrimage to talk to the children and to show them pictures. They could describe how it felt to be part of a group of pilgrims and their feelings when they went to the holy place. How did they show respect to the place?

Watchpoints

W1 *Football supporters wear team colours, jerseys, scarves, etc. People demonstrating wear badges and carry banners. Muslim pilgrims on the Hajj (journey to Makkah) wear plain garments made from white unsewn cloth and no jewellery or perfume.*

Learning outcomes

◆ All should be able to talk about a place which is special to them and to say what makes it special. They should know some ways in which people show membership of a group when travelling together.

◆ Some might be able to describe how they would feel if they visited a special place. They might be able to name some places which are the sites of religious pilgrimage.

◆ A few might be able to describe pilgrims' feelings when visiting a place of religious significance.

Bernadette

Key concepts Belonging, devotion, inspiration

Key words Saint, vision, rosary, belief, faith

Resources ◆ PS29 ◆ Story 'Bernadette of Lourdes' (page 90)

Lourdes

Background

Lourdes is in the Pyrenees (France), situated on a huge rock called Massabielle. It was a small garrison town until 1858, when a young girl saw visions of the Virgin Mary in a grotto. At first religious authorities were sceptical about Bernadette's visions, but during cross-examination she spoke with such authority that her questioners were convinced of her sincerity. The bishop authorised a shrine to be made in the grotto. Bernadette was canonised in 1933 by Pope Pius XI. People with illnesses, disabilities and personal problems visit Lourdes hoping for relief or cure, and there have been reports of success.

Focus: Christianity

Starting points

Tell the story of Bernadette (page 90). Who was the beautiful lady in the story? How do they know? What do they know about her?

Ask the children to imagine Bernadette in the grotto. How did she feel when she saw the lady? How would they feel if a lady like her came and spoke to them while they were by themselves in a lonely place?

Activities

The children could use PS29, colouring, cutting out and sequencing the pictures. They could draw a seventh picture to show what happened next, and write a sentence beneath each picture.

Why didn't Bernadette's parents believe her? What made people believe her in the end? The children could discuss times when people wouldn't believe them. What didn't they believe? How did the children feel? How did they try to convince others? Did it work?

Development

Can the children explain why thousands of people go to Lourdes each year? Talk about faith. Do the children know what it means? Have they touched things for luck?

Watchpoints

 She was the Virgin Mary who, Christians believe, was the mother of Jesus.

 You could invite someone who has been to Lourdes to talk to the children and show them their photographs, slides or souvenirs. The visitor should tell the children what it meant to him or her to visit Lourdes.

Learning outcomes

◆ All should be able to re-tell the story of St Bernadette and say what is special about Lourdes.
◆ Some might be able to describe Bernadette's feelings when she saw her vision and tried to convince others of what she had seen.
◆ A few might be able to describe how pilgrims might feel when they go to Lourdes, and explain what might have convinced people that Bernadette was telling the truth.

Questions

Key concepts Beliefs, ultimate questions

Key words Commemoration, stupa, bodhi tree

Resources ◆ PS30

Special Places for Buddhists

Background

Buddhists have four major pilgrimage sites: the Lumbini Grove in Nepal, where the Buddha was born; Bodh Gaya (also in Nepal), where he became enlightened while sitting beneath a bodhi tree 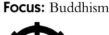; Kusinara in northern India, where he gave his first sermon; and Varanasi (also in northern India), where he died. They visit stupas (shrines) which contain statues and relics of the Buddha.

Focus: Buddhism

Starting points

Ask the children to think of people who have died. What do they or people they know do to keep alive the memory of those who have died? **W2** Discuss any local memorials to people who have died.

Activities

People visit Buddhist pilgrimage sites to try to understand the Buddha's teachings better. The Buddha was enlightened and Buddhists try to find this understanding themselves. **W3** They believe that people can have many lives and that in each life they can understand more and more. They feel that being in these places will help them.

Ask the children to think of questions which are hard to answer. **W4** They could write their questions on the bodhi leaves on PS30. Ask the children to try to answer one of their difficult questions. Where could they sit quietly to think? Is it difficult to think about one question? Remind them about meditating (page 51). After a few minutes' thought they could discuss their question with a friend, then try again to answer it. Emphasise that some questions have no right answer. Let them compare their first and second attempts to answer the question. Did having time for thinking help?

Development

Ask the children to draw and write their ideas of life after death. If they could be reborn, who or what would they like to be?

Watchpoints

W1 *The tree at Bodh Gaya is a descendant of the one under which the Buddha sat. Cuttings from this and its ancestors are considered holy, and are planted at shrines.*

W2 *They might visit/tend their graves; visit places where they lived; look at things they used; look at photographs. Be sensitive to any children who have suffered a bereavement, including the death of a pet.*

W3 *Enlightened means understood what life was for. Buddhists believe in reincarnation. Each incarnation brings with it something from the last. They try to live as good a life as possible to ensure a better rebirth.*

W4 *Questions might be: where is God? what happens when people die? do ghosts exist? why do we have four fingers and a thumb on each hand? where did the air come from? how was the Earth made?*

Learning outcomes

◆ All should know that Buddhists try to find the answers to difficult questions, and that going to special places helps them.

◆ Some might appreciate that thinking and meditating might help them to answer difficult questions.

◆ A few might understand what is meant by reincarnation and be able to express their ideas about it.

Rangoli patterns

Hanukiah

The Dreidl Game

Each group will need some counters and a spinner.

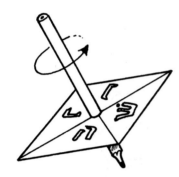

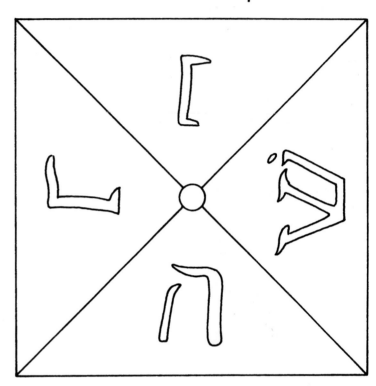

Cut out the spinner.

Push a pencil through the middle.

Put all the counters in a pile.

Set a timer so that you know when to end the game.

Take it in turns to spin the dreidl.

If it lands on [ ] (nun) do nothing.

If it lands on [ ] (gimmel) take all the counters.

If it lands on [ ] (hey) take half the counters.

If it lands on [ ] (shin) put all your counters back on the pile.

STANLEY THORNES
infant RE

The Buddha's Hands

Meditating or concentrating

Giving

Teaching

Protecting

Touching the Earth. Asking the Earth to witness that he has found the meaning of life.

Poems, Songs and Prayers

SOME CHRISTIAN PRAYERS

The Lord's Prayer

Our Father in Heaven, hallowed be your name, your kingdom come, your will be done, on Earth as it is in Heaven. Give us today our daily bread. Forgive us our sins as we forgive those who sin against us. Lead us not into temptation, but deliver us from evil. For the kingdom, the power and the glory are yours. Now and forever. Amen.

The Hail Mary

Hail Mary, full of grace, the Lord is with thee. Blessed art thou among women, and blessed is the fruit of thy womb, Jesus. Holy Mary, Mother of God, pray for us sinners now and at the hour of our death. Amen

The Glory Be

Glory be to the Father, and to the Son, and to the Holy Spirit. As it was in the beginning, is now and ever shall be, world without end. Amen.

PART OF A HINDU PRAYER

We meditate on the lovely sight of Saviti (the Sun god). May it stimulate our thoughts.

Part of the Hindu arti prayer

O Lord of the Universe, supreme soul, dispeller of sorrow, hail to you. May your rule of righteousness be established everywhere, for you banish in an instant the agonies of those who worship you...

A JEWISH PRAYER

The Shema

Hear, O Israel, the Lord our God the Lord is One, and you shall love the Lord your God with all your heart and with all your soul and with all your might.

SIKH PRAYERS

The Mool Mantra (the most important Sikh prayer)

There is only one God; Truth is His name.
He is the Creator; He is without fear.
He is without hate; Immortal and without form.
He is beyond birth and death, the Enlightened One.
He can be known by the Guru's grace.

The Japji (morning prayer)

The True One alone was in the beginning.
The True One is through all ages.
The True One exists now.
The True One shall be for ever.

We Plough the Fields and Scatter (extract)

All good gifts around us
Are sent from Heaven above,
Then thank the Lord,
O thank the Lord,
For all His love.

We thank Thee then, O Father,
For all things bright and good;
The seed-time and the harvest,
Our life, our health, our food.
No gifts have we to offer
For all Thy love imparts,
But that which Thou desirest,
Our humble, thankful hearts.

The End of the Road (from 'The Path to Rome')

In these boots and with this staff
Two hundred leagues and a half
Walked I, went I, paced I, tripped I,
Marched I, held I, skelped I, slipped I,
Pushed I, panted, swung and dashed I;
Picked I, forded, swam and splashed I,
Strolled I, climbed I, crawled and scrambled,
Dropped and dipped I, ranged and rambled;
Plodded I, hobbled I, trudged and tramped I,
And in lonely spinneys camped I,
Lingered, loitered, limped and crept I,
Clambered, halted, stepped and leapt I,
Slowly sauntered, roundly strode I,
And...

Let me not conceal it ... rode I.
(For who but critics could complain
Of 'riding' in a railway train?)

Across the valleys and the high land,
With all the world on either hand,
Drinking when I had a mind to,
Singing when I felt inclined to;
Nor ever turned my face to home
Till I had slaked my heart in Rome.

HILAIRE BELLOC

Stories

THE PARABLE OF THE SOWER

(adapted from Mark 4.3–9, Luke 8.4–9)

Wherever Jesus went people would gather to hear him speak. He sometimes told parables (stories with meanings) which he would explain to them. One day a crowd had gathered by the Sea of Galilee to listen to Jesus teaching the word of God. They were mostly farming people and understood crops and harvests, so he told them a story which they would understand.

Jesus said, 'One day a sower went out into the fields with his sack of seeds. He scattered handfuls of seeds. Some fell on the footpath; the birds ate them. Others fell on rocky ground; they sprouted quickly but their roots were not deep enough and the plants were scorched by the sun: they withered away. Some seeds fell among thistles, which choked the corn. But some of the seeds fell on good soil; they grew into strong healthy plants which could give thirty, sixty, even a hundred times more seed.'

Some people asked Jesus questions about the parable. He told them that the sower sows the word of God.

'Those on the footpath,' he said, 'are people in whom the word is sown, but as soon as they hear it they forget it. It is the same for those on rocky ground; they might hear the word with joy, but it does not take root in them, and as soon as things get difficult they forget all about it. Those among the thistles hear the word, but are too fond of things which money can buy; all kinds of evils choke the word of God. But those in the good soil hear the word and welcome it. They take notice of it and repay God thirty, sixty, even a hundred times over, and they spread the word among that many people.'

Points to discuss:

- *How can we tell that Jesus was special?*
- *Where did the seeds grow best? Why?*
- *Why didn't the other seeds grow?*
- *Which people help spread the word of God?*
- *Why do some people take no notice of God's word?*

RAMA AND SITA

(adapted from the story in the Ramayana)

Dasharata was the king of Ayodhya. He had three wives but no children. He wanted children so much that he asked the god Agni to help him. Agni gave him a magic potion for his wives – Kausalya, Sumitra and Kaikeyi. Soon Kausalya had a son, Rama, Sumitra gave birth to Lakshaman and Shatrughna, and Kaikeyi had a son, Bharata.

Points to discuss:

- *What is a curse?*
- *Why did Dasharata send Rama away even though he didn't want to?*
- *Who are the good characters in this story?*
- *Who are the bad characters?*
- *How can we tell they are bad?*

King Dasharata was a keen hunter and a good shot with a bow and arrow. One day, when he was out hunting deer, he heard a rustling in some bushes, quickly took aim and shot an arrow. The rustling stopped. Dasharata went to look for the deer he had shot. He parted the branches, but there on the ground was a little boy with an arrow through his heart. The boy's mother and father put a dreadful curse on Dasharata: 'You shall die, like us, grieving for your dead son,' and then, because the shock was too great to bear, they died.

Dasharata had an important battle to fight against his enemies; but his grief was so great that he could not face it. One of his wives, Kaikeyi, urged him to face the enemy. 'You will win the battle,' she said. 'Go and fight.' Dasharata won the battle, and as a reward he promised Kaikeyi that she could have any two wishes she wanted. She waited for many years, until the king's eldest son, Rama, had grown up to be a wise young man and a great warrior, and had married Sita.

Kaikeyi was jealous because her own son, Bharata, who was younger than Rama, would not become the next king. Now she went to Dasharata and said, 'You once promised me two wishes. Now I want you to make Bharata your heir and to send Rama away.' Dasharata did not know what to do: he could not bear to send Rama away, but a promise was a promise.

The people of Ayodhya tried to persuade the king to let Rama and Sita stay, but he knew he must keep his word. With tears in his eyes he said goodbye to them: 'The curse of the dead boy's parents is coming true,' he thought.

In the forest Ravana, an evil demon with many heads, saw Sita. He wanted to take her away and waited for Rama to go off hunting and leave her on her own. When Rama set off he drew a magic circle on the ground. 'Do not step outside this circle and you will be safe,' he said to Sita. 'I shall be back as soon as I have got enough food for us.'

Sita stayed in the circle, watching the animals in the forest. Then she saw a beautiful golden deer which was limping. 'I must help it!' she cried. But to get close to it she had to leave the circle. At that moment Ravana appeared. He seized Sita and carried her away to his castle on the island of Lanka.

Rama came back. Sita had gone. Where was she? Rama had a great friend, the Monkey King, who knew everything which happened in the woods; and he called on him for help. 'Have no fear,' said the Monkey King. 'The monkeys will help us to find Sita and bring her back safely.'

The monkeys joined themselves together to form a bridge across the sea to Lanka. The Monkey King went across with Rama and the rest of the monkeys. There was a fierce battle between the

Points to discuss:
- *Did anything unfair happen in this story?*
- *Why was it unfair?*

81

demon Ravana and Rama with his monkey army. Many monkeys were killed. Finally Rama shot the evil demon with an arrow. Sita was safe. Rama never forgot the help the monkeys had given him. On some Hindu temples you will see pictures of monkeys, which are in memory of this story.

Rama and Sita now went back to Ayodhya, travelling through the dark night. The Monkey King had sent a message to the people there to tell them the good news. The people all rejoiced and put lights in their windows to help Rama and Sita to find their way and to welcome them home. The lights were called divas.

JUDAS MACCABAEUS AND THE TEMPLE

About 3,000 years ago in the land of Israel, King Solomon built the first Temple, in Jerusalem, for the Jews. It was their holy place and to show that God was there a special oil lamp was kept burning night and day.

The Syrians saw the crops which the Jews were growing and wanted this good land; their king sent an army to capture Israel. Mattathias led the Jews into a fierce battle. After a long struggle they won, but Mattathias knew that more soldiers would come – perhaps too many for the Jews to beat the next time. So he and his people hid in caves in the hills and made bows and arrows. Soon the Syrian soldiers arrived near Jerusalem. At night the Jews would make surprise attacks on them.

The war went on for two years. Mattathias was injured in the fighting and knew that he would soon die. He called together his five sons and told one of them, called Judas, that he must be the Maccabee, the leader of the Jewish people, and lead them into battle against the Syrians. Judas did as his father had told him. His people drove out the enemy and were able to go back to their homes.

The Jews felt excited and happy as they went back into Jerusalem. They could see their beloved Temple: they would go straight there to worship God and to give thanks for their victory. But as they went into the Temple they felt that something was not right: the special light had gone out and the Temple had a dirty smell. The building was full of rubbish and filth, the stonework had been damaged and the beautiful curtains had been torn. 'We must clean up the Temple, make it holy again and then light the lamp,' they thought. They brushed and shovelled and scrubbed, polished and mended. They said prayers to ask God to bless the Temple and make it holy again. The lamp had to be lit. But the Syrians had used up all the oil.

The Jews searched and searched. Someone found an oil jar. They tipped it up and found just one drop of oil. That would not last very long. More oil must be fetched.

Points to discuss:

◆ *Why did the Temple have a special light?*
◆ *Why did the Jews want to light the lamp as soon as they could?*
◆ *What miracle happened in the story?*
◆ *How must the Jews have felt when they re-lit the lamp?*
◆ *How do Jews commemorate the miracle?*

A messenger set off, but the journey would take him four days there and another four days back. The small drop of oil would never last for eight days, but the lamp must be lit. There was a great celebration as the lamp was lit: psalms and hymns were sung and then there was a feast. The flame was still burning at the end of the evening. The next morning it was still burning. Each day the flame kept on burning and it seemed to be getting brighter. It was a miracle.

On the eighth day the messenger sped into Jerusalem with the oil. He thought the lamp must have burned out. He rubbed his eyes, then looked again at the lamp: yes, it was still burning! 'It is a miracle,' the people said to him. 'The lamp has burned for eight days, and there was only a small drop of oil in it.'

Today every synagogue, like the Temple, has a light which is never allowed to go out. Nowadays these lights are electric, but Jews celebrate the victory of Judas Maccabaeus by lighting eight candles on a special holder called a hanukiah.

THE WOMAN IN THE CROWD AND JAIRUS' DAUGHTER

(adapted from Luke 8.40–56)

The news was spreading fast that Jesus could heal sick people; an important man called Jairus had heard about him and wanted him to heal his little girl, who was very sick. Jairus pushed his way through the crowd around Jesus and knelt in front of him. 'Please come,' he cried, 'My little girl is very sick.' Jesus followed him and as they made their way through the throng of people a woman reached out and just managed to touch the hem of Jesus' cloak.

'That will be enough,' the woman said to herself, 'I have touched his clothing. I shall be cured of my bleeding.' She had an illness which had made her bleed inside for many years. At the moment she touched Jesus' cloak she felt that the bleeding had stopped.

Suddenly Jesus halted and said, 'Who touched my cloak?'

His disciples said, 'There are always people touching you in this crowd: look at them pushing to be near you.'

Jesus said, 'Someone touched me. I felt power going out of me.' He looked around, and a very frightened woman stepped slowly towards him and went down on her knees. Trembling, she told him what she had done. Jesus looked at her with tender eyes and said, 'Your faith has cured you.'

While Jesus was talking to the woman, Jairus' servant arrived. Jairus knew at once that his daughter had died. 'Don't waste Jesus' time,' said the servant, 'It is too late now.'

Point to discuss:

- *What do the children think it means to have faith in someone or something?*
- *What have they seen people doing which shows that they have faith?*
- *What would the people in the crowd have thought when Jesus said that he felt someone touch the hem of his cloak?*
- *What would they have thought and said when the woman was cured?*
- *Do the children ever do anything which they believe might help them – such as touching special things or keeping special things with them?*
- *Talk about superstitions and 'lucky charms'. How was the woman's faith in Jesus different from this? (She believed that Jesus was special and could help her without even seeing her, so long as she had faith.)*

Jesus overheard these words and turned to Jairus. 'Have faith,' he said, then he hurried to Jairus' house. Everyone was crying. 'Go outside and be quiet,' Jesus said to them, 'She is sleeping, not dead.' Some of the neighbours laughed, but they did as Jesus told them. The only people Jesus allowed in the house were Jairus and his wife, and three of his disciples: Simon Peter, James and John.

Jesus walked towards the little girl's bed and gently took her hand. 'Get up from your bed,' he said softly. She opened her eyes, blinked and sat up. Then she got up and went to her parents. 'Now give her something to eat,' said Jesus.

ST FRANCIS OF ASSISI

Giovanni Bernadone was born in Assisi in Italy in 1181, more than eight hundred years ago. His family was very rich and he enjoyed himself, buying expensive clothes and fine horses. He loved excitement and went to look for adventure as a soldier. Because of his knowledge of French and love of French songs, Giovanni was nicknamed *Il Francesco*, which means 'the little Frenchman' (Francis in English).

One day Francis saw a man begging by the roadside. Francis was about to ride past when he recognised the man; the beggar had been from a wealthy family, like himself. 'What has happened to him?' he wondered. He thought of his own riches, and decided that he must use them to help people. He took off his fine coat and gave it to the beggar.

Francis began to have dreams; in his dreams God was telling him to give up his rich lifestyle and to use his money to help people. He left his fine home and gave away all his riches to help poor people. He no longer wore beautiful clothes; his shirt was rough and scratchy and his feet were bare. He no longer ate expensive foods: he became a begger and ate whatever people gave him. Francis was sure that God would provide all that he needed; he had no need to keep any of his riches.

One day Francis went into an old ruined church in Assisi. He heard God's voice saying, 'Francis, re-build my church. It has no walls but the air and no roof but the sky.' God did not mean just that church, but people's belief in him. Francis knew he must find others who believed in God as he did; he gathered a group of faithful followers. Together they founded a monastery in Assisi. Men went there to be monks, to serve God through helping others, and to worship God. Now there are Franciscan monasteries all over the world.

There are stories which show how animals could see Francis's goodness. One story tells of a town whose people were attacked by a killer wolf. Francis set off to find it. The wolf was lurking in the woods near the town; when Francis saw it he spoke to it gently, and it padded softly behind him, back to the town. The townspeople

Points to discuss:

◆ *What special things did St Francis do, which made him a saint?*

◆ *What did Francis see which made him decide to change his way of life? Talk about the other ways in which he might have reacted to the beggar.*

◆ *How did he change?*

◆ *What difficulties might he have faced? (Talk about doing without luxuries and even necessities.)*

~~~~~~

would not go near Francis and the wolf. He said, 'My friends, this wolf will not harm you. It is hungry, that's all. Why don't you feed it?' From that day the people fed the wolf, and it never harmed anyone again.

THE BIRTH OF MOSES

A baby boy lay smiling in his mother's arms. She tried to smile back at him but all she could think of was the danger which faced her baby. She was an Israelite, and at that time the Israelites were slaves in Egypt. The pharaoh, who ruled Egypt, had been getting worried when he saw that the number of Israelites was growing. Soon they would outnumber his own people. He told his soldiers to throw the Israelite baby boys into the Nile but to spare the girls. The mother hid her baby from the Egyptians for three months. At last she thought up a plan; she made a basket from rushes, and waterproofed it with tar, then she set off to the river with her daughter and the baby. She knew that Pharaoh's daughter bathed in the river each day. She put the baby in the basket and carefully hid it in the bulrushes near the river bank. The basket floated, out of sight, among the rushes. 'Hide yourself nearby and watch,' she said to her daughter.

Pharaoh's daughter soon appeared with her ladies-in-waiting. She told them to walk along the bank while she bathed in the river. Her servant girl stayed nearby. Before long Pharaoh's daughter spotted the basket floating among the bulrushes. She sent her servant-girl to fetch it. 'Why, it's a little Israelite baby!' she exclaimed, as she looked inside it. She knew he would be killed if the guards found him unless somebody protected him. She took pity on the crying baby, whose sister was watching and listening close by. The girl came down to the river and asked Pharaoh's daughter, 'Shall I find an Israelite woman to nurse the baby?' Pharaoh's daughter agreed – and guess whom the girl asked to look after the baby? Her mother, the baby's mother! Pharaoh's daughter told the woman that she would pay her to nurse the child until he was old enough to go and live with her in the royal palace.

When Moses was old enough his mother took him along to Pharaoh's daughter, who adopted him. And so an Israelite baby grew up in the pharaoh's palace.

BILAL

Bilal lifted his head from his work in the fields near Makkah. He listened. 'One God. Only one God,' cried a voice. It sounded like Ammar, one of the other slaves; he would be whipped for disagreeing with Umaya, their master. Umaya worshipped many gods and he had told all his slaves that they must do the same. Most of them did – it was better than being whipped; but now Ammar had dared to speak out.

Point to discuss:

- ◆ *Why did the pharaoh want to kill the Israelite baby boys?*
- ◆ *How did Moses' mother manage to keep him with her while he was a baby?*
- ◆ *Talk about the cleverness of Moses' mother: she saved his life but managed to keep him with her while he was a baby.*
- ◆ *Do the children think Moses would have a better life with Pharaoh's daughter than with his own family? Why/why not? How would it be different?*

Points to discuss:

- ◆ *What sort of character was Bilal?*
- ◆ *How can we tell?*
- ◆ *Some children may be able to write character studies of Bilal.*
- ◆ *Talk about the ways in which some people think they are better than others.*

Then Umaya appeared in the field; Bilal quickly got on with his work, but Umaya came towards him, carrying a whip. Bilal could feel his heart beating so fast that he thought his chest would burst. 'Slave,' said Umaya, 'I have a job for you. Take this whip and give that trouble-maker a good thrashing. That will teach him a lesson.'

Bilal took the whip and walked into the courtyard of Umaya's great house. There was Ammar, held in chains by two guards, calling out for all he was worth, 'There is one God. Everybody is equal. Nobody is better than anyone else.' Bilal thought about these words. 'He is right,' he said to himself. He dropped the whip to the ground. The other slaves watched in silence, holding their breath. 'No, I will not whip him,' said Bilal, 'There *is* one God, and everybody is equal.'

Umaya was furious. He ordered the guards to throw Bilal to the ground and pile great heavy rocks on him. 'That will make him quiet,' growled Umaya. Only the top of Bilal's head, feet and hands showed under the pile of rocks, from which came the sound of his voice, calling 'Only one God. There is only one God.'

A follower of the prophet Muhammad (pbuh), Abu Bakr, came along to see what all the commotion was about. He stopped when he saw Bilal: 'Umaya,' he said, 'How can you treat another human being in this way?'

Umaya replied, 'He is my slave. I bought him. I can do what I want with him. If you buy him, you can do what you want with him.'

'Yes, I shall buy him,' said Abu Bakr. He gently lifted the rocks off Bilal, and carried him back to his home. From that day Bilal became a follower of the Prophet.

After that the Prophet's followers decided to build a place where they could worship God. How would they tell people when to come to pray? They thought about different ways to call the people: a drum, a bell, a trumpet, or perhaps a horn. They could not decide, until one of them, Abdullah, told the others of a dream in which he heard a voice calling people to worship. It was a clear, loud voice, and everyone who heard it came to pray. That was the answer, but whose voice should it be?

Muhammad looked at Bilal. 'Yours shall be the voice which calls the people of Makkah to prayer,' he said. 'Yours is the voice which praised God from under a pile of rocks.'

'But what shall I call?' asked Bilal.

'Praise God,' said the Prophet. 'Say that Muhammad is his messenger, and call the people to prayer.' So Bilal climbed up on to the roof of the building. He had an important job to do. He had to do it well. He took a deep breath, threw back his head and called the words which are still used to call Muslims to prayer to this day: 'Allahu Akbar. God is most great. I bear witness that there is no God but Allah and that Muhammad is his messenger. Come to prayer. Allah is most great.'

GURU NANAK

Guru Nanak was born more than five hundred years ago in 1469. In the part of India where he lived there were often arguments between Hindus and Muslims about religion. Guru Nanak did not think it mattered how people worshipped God, as long as they felt right about it and as long as they loved God.

Nanak spent time alone in peaceful places, thinking about God and composing beautiful songs which he would sing to worship God. He called himself God's minstrel. People would look for him to listen to his songs; one man called Mardana used to meet him often to sing and play music to God, and gradually more people joined them. Nanak used to wash in the river before he sang to God; this was his way of making himself clean before doing something holy. Mardana used to look after his clothes on the riverbank.

One day Mardana was worried. Nanak had been under the water for a long time; had he drowned? He called for help, and the people who had come to sing with Nanak waded into the river. They could not find him. Mardana was so sad that he sat next to Nanak's clothes on the bank for three days.

On the third day, Mardana had a wonderful surprise; out of the river walked Nanak, as if nothing had happened. Everyone rejoiced, but Nanak would not talk about his time in the river. He sat alone thinking, meditating. Then he began to give away all his things: fine clothes, furniture, everything. His faithful followers wondered what had happened to him.

Then Nanak told his friends what had happened while he was under the water. He had been to a beautiful place, to meet God. Someone had given him a special sweet drink, amrit, which means nectar, and then God had asked him to sing some of his songs.

After that Nanak began to travel so that he could teach more people about God through his songs. He took no money with him, but lived on whatever people gave him; he slept wherever someone gave him shelter. After twenty years of travelling Guru Nanak went to live in the Punjab in northern India. Sikhs today still sing Guru Nanak's songs when they praise God.

Points to discuss:
◆ *How can we tell Guru Nanak was special?*
◆ *What made people want to worship with Guru Nanak?*
◆ *How did people know that he had been with God?*
◆ *How did his time under the water change him?*
◆ *In what ways was Guru Nanak like St Francis?*

GURU NANAK'S SONG

I was a minstrel out of work,
The Lord gave me employment.
The Mighty One told me, 'Night and day, sing My praise'.
The Lord called the minstrel to His high court.

He put on me the robe of honouring Him and singing His praise.
He gave me the nectar in a cup, the nectar of His true and holy name.
Those who at the bidding of the guru feast and fill themselves
With the Lord's holiness gain peace and joy.
Your minstrel spreads Your glory by singing Your word.
Nanak, through adoring truth we reach the All-Highest.

(Guru Granth Sahib, 150)

THE FIRST BAISAKHI

Baisakhi is the spring festival of Hindus and Sikhs. Guru Gobind
called all his followers to a special meeting on Baisakhi day in
1699. Thousands came from all over India to the Punjab, where
Guru Gobind gave a talk about their faith. Then he called out,
holding up his sword, 'Which of you will die for your faith?' The
crowd went very quiet.

The guru looked at them and said, 'If you will die for your faith,
then come with me into the tent.'

The crowd was still very quiet, then a man stood up and said, 'I
shall die for my faith.' He went into the tent with Guru Gobind.
The people listened and waited. They heard a sword swishing,
then they heard a cry, and then a thud, as if something heavy had
fallen to the ground. Everyone gasped, and some screamed when
Guru Gobind came out of the tent. He held up his sword; it was
dripping with blood. 'Who will be next to die for his faith?' he
called.

Nobody spoke, then: 'I shall,' said another man, and into the tent
he went. The people were silent. Again they heard a sword
swishing, followed by a cry, and then a thud, as if something heavy
had fallen to the ground. Again the guru came out with his sword
dripping with blood. One by one five men went into the tent.

Then the guru pulled back the flap of the tent. There were the five
men alive. 'Look at the Panj Piare – the Five Faithful Ones,' cried
the guru.

Guru Gobind then made a special mixture of water and sugar. He
stirred it with his double-edged sword. He called the mixture
amrit, which means nectar, and said a prayer to bless it. He
sprinkled some amrit over the Panj Piare. They drank some of it; so
did many of the others who were there, as a sign that they would
follow the teaching of the gurus.

Then Guru Gobind told them some rules which they should obey
and promises which they should make in order to be good Sikhs.
He told the women to have the name Kaur, which means princess,
and the men to have the name Singh, which means lion. Guru
Gobind Singh told the people to be proud of their faith and to
show this by wearing five symbols: the Five Ks.

Points to discuss:

◆ *Talk about volunteering. If people are asked to volunteer for something nice, what happens?*

◆ *What happens if people are asked to volunteer for something difficult or unpleasant?*

THE STORY OF PRINCE SIDDHARTHA GAUTAMA

Prince Siddhartha Gautama was born nearly 2,600 years ago in Lumbini, in Nepal. At his naming ceremony a religious man told his father that he could see a great future for the baby boy: he would become either a great king or a religious teacher. His father wanted him to grow up to be a good man; so he kept him in the royal palace to make sure he did not see any of the evil things in the world. Prince Siddhartha grew up; his parents found a wife for him, but he had still never been outside the grounds of the palace.

Siddhartha longed to see what was outside in the great wide world, and so he set off in the king's chariot with his servant driving. Before long they saw an old man; he was leaning on a stick and every step seemed to take all his strength. 'What is wrong with him?' asked Siddhartha, who had never seen old people.

The servant replied, 'He is suffering because his body is worn out. It happens to everyone who lives to a great age.'

Further on there was what seemed to be just a bundle of rags at the side of the road, but then it moved and groaned. An arm, then a leg, appeared. Siddhartha looked more closely; he saw that the flesh was diseased. He turned to the servant for an answer. 'She is suffering because she is ill,' he said.

Near the river there was a group of people by a great pile of wood. There was a body on top, wrapped in white cloth. Someone set the wood on fire and there was a sweet smell of sandalwood. 'Death,' said the servant. 'Suffering.'

Further on Siddhartha saw a man sitting crosslegged on a small mat. He was wearing just a small piece of cloth around the lower part of his body. Prince Siddhartha could see the bones of his skull and his ribs under his skin; his arms were so thin that they looked as if they would snap. 'He is a holy man,' said the servant. 'He hardly ever sleeps; he spends his time thinking about the meaning of life. He eats just enough to keep himself alive.'

'There has to be an answer to all this suffering,' said Siddhartha. He travelled all over India looking for the answer. He tried living in the same way as the holy man, but he became too weak to think. 'I need to find a middle way,' he said to himself. 'It will be somewhere in between starving like a holy man and living like a prince, as I once did.'

After long travels Prince Siddhartha went back to Nepal. There he sat beneath the branches of a bodhi tree; he thought and thought about life. He began to understand. These are the answers which he found; they are the Four Noble Truths of Buddhism:

> All life has suffering. Suffering comes from people wanting things. Suffering stops when people stop wanting things. Follow the Middle Way.

Points to discuss:

- *Have the children seen people suffering in the same ways as the people in the story; through sickness, old age, or someone dying?*
- *Have they seen any other sorts of suffering, caused by other people? How do people make each other suffer?*
- *What rules would help to stop people suffering?*
- *Talk about the ways in which Prince Siddhartha changed.*
- *In what ways were there changes like those of St Francis and Guru Nanak?*

GANESHA

There was once a lovely goddess called Parvati. She had no children and this made her very sad. She would often say to her husband, the great god Shiva, 'Please let me have a little boy of my own.' But Shiva was always too busy looking after the world to listen to her.

In the end the lonely goddess decided to make a little boy for herself. While she was in the bath she collected all the little flakes of skin and bits of soap which floated on the water after she had washed herself, and squashed them all together. She made a dough from them, and out of this she shaped a little boy. Then she breathed life into him; he became a real baby boy. She called him Ganesha.

Ganesha grew up to be a very good little boy who always did as his mother asked. He had never seen Shiva, who had been away from home for many years, doing important work. One day while Parvati was in the bath a man came to their home. Ganesha ran out to protect his mother from danger. 'Keep out!' cried Ganesha. It was Shiva. He was furious; who was this boy who wouldn't let him into his own home? He took out his sword and sliced off Ganesha's head.

Parvati came rushing out to see what was going on. She screamed when she saw Shiva with his sword out and Ganesha lying on the ground. She told Shiva the story of Ganesha. Shiva promised to get a new head for Ganesha and to bring him back to life. 'I'll get the head of the first animal I see,' he said.

The first animal he saw in the forest was an elephant. The great hunter, Shiva, had no trouble capturing the enormous animal and cutting off its head. He took home the elephant's head and fixed it on to Ganesha's body.

Parvati was so pleased to have Ganesha alive again that she didn't mind that he had an elephant's head. She gave him a hug and every time she looked at him she liked his big ears and his trunk more and more. She was pleased, too, that now Shiva had helped to make him.

BERNADETTE OF LOURDES

Bernadette Soubirous lived in France, in a place called Lourdes. She was born in 1844 into a very poor family who lived in one small room. To help her parents, Bernadette used to go with her sister and her friend to collect firewood. One cold winter's day they were gathering firewood by the river at Massabielle when Bernadette felt even colder than usual. She huddled inside her cloak, but she was still cold, and her asthma was making her chest hurt. She wished Jeanne and Toinette would come back. She wanted to go home.

Points to discuss:

◆ *Why did the lady appear only when Bernadette was there?*
◆ *Why did nobody else see her?*
◆ *What would the children think if one of their friends told them that he or she had talked to a lady like the one in the story?*
◆ *What made people believe Bernadette's story?*

90

It was a still, calm day, but a sudden rush of wind startled Bernadette. The trees were quite still, but there it was again, the sound of rushing wind. She looked up towards a cave in the rock. There, in front of the cave, the only thing which moved was one bush; it seemed as if a gale were tossing its branches. Then a golden cloud seemed to come out of the cave.

Bernadette held her breath. She blinked and looked again; a beautiful lady wearing a white dress and veil was by the cave. She had yellow roses on her feet and rosary beads over her arm. Bernadette took out her own rosary. She wanted to pray. She tried to make the sign of the cross but her arm seemed too heavy to move. The lady made the sign of the cross; Bernadette's arm moved at the same time. With the beautiful lady she said the rosary. At the end of it the lady had gone.

Bernadette could not move from the spot until Jeanne and Toinette came back. She was so pale they thought she was ill. She asked them if they had ever seen anything strange in the cave, but they said, 'No. Why? What have you seen?' Bernadette told them about the lady. They looked up toward the cave. Nothing. They looked at Bernadette's shining eyes and they knew something special had happened to her.

When Bernadette and Toinette reached home their mother asked what was wrong with Bernadette. She could not speak, so Toinette told their mother about the lady in the cave. Madame Soubirous was very angry. 'What rubbish!' she said. 'I don't want to hear another word of it; and you must keep away from that cave. There will be trouble if I catch you going there again. Beautiful lady indeed!'

Bernadette longed to go back to the cave. She became paler and paler. On the third day her mother was so worried about her that she gave in. Bernadette ran to the cave and went down on her knees to pray. Sure enough the lady came again. This happened every day. Bernadette felt happier there than she felt anywhere else.

One day the lady told Bernadette to drink from a spring in the cave. Bernadette had never seen a spring there, but she dug with her hands in the place to which the lady pointed. She felt water under the rocky soil. Yes, there was a spring!

Soon the news of Bernadette's lady began to spread. People came and watched her praying with the lady, but only Bernadette saw her. People believed that the spring was holy, and one woman brought her little boy who had an eye disease. She bathed his eyes in the water from the spring; he was healed.

Some people laughed at Bernadette, and she was questioned by the police about the lady in the cave. She always answered in a quiet, gentle way. Her eyes shone with truth and her whole face was radiant as she told them about the lady.

Bernadette went to live as a nun in a convent in Nevers; but she had never had good health, and she died when she was only 35. The little cave at Massabielle now has a shrine to the lady and a statue of Bernadette. The lady had told Bernadette to have a church built at the cave. There are three churches now, and a large open place with room for great crowds of people to pray. There is a busy railway station where people arrive from all over the world, many of them with illnesses or disabilities which they believe will be cured. They say that going to that special shrine makes them feel comforted.

Extra Background Information

Christian Wedding

The priest tells the man and woman that the purpose of marriage is to bring up children. They declare that there is no reason why they cannot marry, such as being too closely related or having a husband or wife already. All those at the service are asked to say if they know of any reason why the couple should not marry, or else for ever hold their peace. The couple make vows and exchange rings (see 'Christian [Anglican] wedding' below).

Sikh Wedding

Everyone is given karah parshad (a sweet food which has been blessed). The ceremony usually begins with a prayer. Then the bride and groom sit in front of the Guru Granth Sahib and might give one another garlands of flowers. After the granthi (the person who will read from the holy book) has made a short speech about the importance of marriage in the community and about the responsibilities of marriage, the couple walk clockwise round the Guru Granth Sahib, while everyone recites the wedding hymn, the Lavaan. During the last verse the guests scatter petals in front of the couple.

Wedding Symbols

Many of the symbols traditionally associated with Christian marriage have no religious basis and some have pagan origins: a ring has no start or end and so is a symbol of eternity (the couple promise to stay together for life), confetti or rice symbolises fertility because the wedding service encourages the couple to have children, white is a symbol of purity to show that the bride has not been married before, flowers symbolise life, and the top layer of the wedding cake is often preserved to be used as a christening cake for the couple's first child.

A Sikh bride usually wears red, which is considered lucky (in Sikhism, as in Hinduism, white is the colour of mourning). She will wear a lot of gold jewellery, including chains which hang from nose to ear, and her dress is likely to be richly embroidered. The bridegroom wears a pink or red turban.

Christian (Anglican) wedding

The words 'ye', 'thee' and 'thou' have been changed to 'you'. '[ ]' denotes words added for explanation to children.)

Minister: I ... charge you both, as you will answer at the ... day of judgement when the secrets of all hearts shall be disclosed, that if either of you know any impediment [reason] why you may not be lawfully joined together in matrimony, you do now confess it ...

Minister: Will you have this woman to your wedded wife, to live together according to God's law in the holy estate of Matrimony? Will you love her, comfort her, honour and keep her, in sickness and in health? and, forsaking all other, keep yourself only unto her, so long as you both shall live? The man shall answer: I will. Minister: Will you have this man to your wedded husband, to live together according to God's law in the holy estate of Matrimony? Will you love him, comfort him, honour and keep him, in sickness and in health? and, forsaking all other, keep yourself only for him, so long as you both shall live? The woman shall answer: I will. The man repeats after the minister: I ... take you ... to my wedded wife, to have and to hold from this day forward, for better, for worse: for richer, for poorer; in sickness and in health; to love and to cherish, till death us do part, according to God's holy law; and thereto I give you my troth [promise]. The woman repeats after the minister: I ... take you ... to my wedded husband, to have and to hold from this day forward, for better for worse: for richer, for poorer; in sickness and in health; to love and to cherish, till death us do part, according to God's holy law; and thereto I give you my troth [promise].

Wesak

Wesak commemorates the main events in the life of the Buddha (his birth, enlightenment and death) which took place in different years some 2,500 years ago. It is celebrated in May, but the exact date varies.

During Wesak many Buddhists reflect on the past year and make resolutions for the following year. They might meditate, trying to push bad thoughts out of their minds and to think only good thoughts. They might give presents or money to people in need.

Buddhists in different parts of the world celebrate Wesak differently: in Japan they wash statues of the Buddha with scented water; in Sri Lanka they decorate their homes and streets with lanterns; in Thailand they clean their homes and statues of the Buddha, and hang up flags, streamers and garlands of flowers, release caged birds and have candle-lit processions. Many Buddhists send one another greetings cards featuring lanterns, candles, garlands of flowers, the lotus flower, elephants, and the bodhi tree under which the Buddha became enlightened (see Unit 2, Lesson 10). They might go to a vihara (temple) where monks read from the scriptures; they usually give alms to the monks on this, the most important day of the year. Buddhists revere the Buddha as the founder of their faith; they do not worship him. Wesak is a commemorative festival, but not a feast day; no special foods are eaten.

The Temple

The Temple is of great importance to Jews. Jewish scriptures tell of the occasions on which enemies of the Jews destroyed the Temple; each time the Jews rebuilt it. The building of the first Tabernacle by Moses is described in Exodus 40, then the first Temple in Jerusalem, by Solomon, in about 1000 BCE (1 Kings 6). The Babylonians destroyed it. The second Temple was built, only to be destroyed by the Romans in 70 CE. All that remains of it is the Western Wall. There are two fasts which mourn the destruction of the temple Yom Hashoah and Tisha B'Ar.

The Sermon on the Mount

(adapted from Matthew 5.38–47)

Jesus said to the people, 'Do not set yourself against people who do you wrong; if someone slaps you on the right cheek, turn the left cheek to him or her; if people want to take your shirt, offer them your coat too. You have learned to love your neighbour: love your enemy too. If you love only those who love you, what reward can you expect?'

The Beatitudes

(adapted from Matthew 5.3–10)

How blest are those who know their need of God;
   the kingdom of Heaven is theirs.

How blest are the sorrowful;
   they shall find consolation.

How blest are those of a gentle spirit;
   they shall have the Earth for their possession.

How blest are those who hunger and thirst to see right prevail;
   they shall be satisfied.

How blest are those who show mercy;
   mercy shall be shown to them.

How blest are those whose hearts are pure;
   they shall see God.

How blest are the peacemakers;
   God shall call them his sons.

How blest are those who have suffered persecution for the cause of right;
   the kingdom of Heaven is theirs.

The Adhan (The Call to Prayer)

The Adhan in Arabic (transliterated):

Allahu Akbar Ashhadu an la ilaha illallah Ashhadu anna muhammadar rasulullah Hayya alas salah. Allahu Akbar.

The Adhan in English:

Allah is most great. I bear witness that there is no god but Allah and that Muhammad is his messenger. Come to prayer. Allah is most great.

Puja

The preparations for puja, which are carried out before prayers begin, are referred to as the arti ceremony. The puja tray usually has on it:

- flowers, to beautify the surroundings and give a pleasant smell;
- a dish of rice grains, nuts, sweets or fruit, which are blessed and offered to the murtis and, after worship, shared among the worshippers as parshad (blessed food);
- kum kum or sandalwood paste or turmeric, to put a spot on the forehead of the deity, symbolising wisdom;
- a dish of milk, to offer to the murtis and then, after worship, to share among the worshippers;
- a spoon, to offer the milk or water to the murtis;
- a pot of water, to wash the faces of the murtis before worship (it might also be sprinkled over the murtis and, after puja, the worshippers might drink any which remains);
- incense sticks, to purify the atmosphere in the home or temple and to perfume the air before worship;
- a bell, to ring at the beginning of puja to announce to the deity that worship is about to begin;
- a diva, which is lit at the beginning of puja.

Religious Festivals Chart

	Christian	Jewish	Muslim	Hindu	Sikh	Buddhist
JANUARY	Epiphany					
FEBRUARY			Ramadan			
MARCH	Lent / Easter	Purim / Pesach	Id ul-Fitr	Holi		
APRIL					Baisakhi	
MAY	Pentecost					Wesak
JUNE						
JULY						
AUGUST						
SEPTEMBER		Rosh Hashanah Yom Kippur Sukkot				
OCTOBER				Divali		
NOVEMBER					Guru Nanak's Birthday	
DECEMBER	Advent Christmas	Hanukkah				

Many religious festivals do not fall on the same day every year, but move according to the phase of the moon or other factors, thus the dates on this chart are only approximate.

STANLEY THORNES

infant RE

An overview of the coverage of the six major religions

Book 1

			RELIGIOUS FOCUS					
			General	Buddhism	Christianity	Hinduism	Islam	Judaism	Sikhism
UNIT 1: Myself	1	Who am I?	•						•
	2	How do I Feel?	•						
	3	At Home						•	
	4	My Family				•			
	5	My Day					•		
	6	My Friends			•			•	
	7	Jesus' Friends			•				
	8	Thinking of Others					•		•
	9	Belonging							•
	10	A Special Baby – The Christmas Story			•				
UNIT 2: New Life	1	The Creation			•			•	
	2	Caring for the Environment			•		•	•	
	3	Hurt no Living Thing		•					
	4	The Seasons	•						
	5	Life Cycles		•	•				
	6	Growing Things	•						
	7	Babies			•	•			
	8	Holi				•			
	9	The Story of Easter			•				
	10	Easter Customs and Symbols			•				
UNIT 3: Special Books	1	I Like Books	•						
	2	Telling Stories	•						
	3	Religious Books	•						
	4	The Bible			•				
	5	Jesus Calms the Storm			•				
	6	Jesus Heals a Blind Man			•				
	7	The Torah						•	
	8	Moses and the Ten Commandments						•	
	9	Muhammad (pbuh), God's Messenger					•		
	10	The Qur'an					•		

Book 2

			RELIGIOUS FOCUS						
			General	Buddhism	Christianity	Hinduism	Islam	Judaism	Sikhism
UNIT 1: Special Times	1	'Milestones'	●						
	2	Harvest			●				
	3	A Shared Meal							●
	4	Names and Threads				●			
	5	Wedding			●				●
	6	Wesak		●					
	7	Divali				●			
	8	Hanukkah						●	
	9	Id ul-Fitr					●		
	10	Advent			●				
UNIT 2: Special People	1	Special People in the Community	●						
	2	Anglican Minister			●				
	3	Jesus the Healer			●				
	4	Jesus the Teacher			●				
	5	St Francis			●				
	6	Moses						●	
	7	The Mu'adhin					●		
	8	Guru Nanak							●
	9	Guru Gobind Singh							●
	10	The Buddha		●					
UNIT 3: Special Places	1	A Stone Circle	●						
	2	Special Places in the Community	●						
	3	A Place for Prayer			●	●		●	●
	4	Worshipping at Home			●	●			
	5	Cathedral			●				
	6	Synagogue						●	
	7	Doorways				●			
	8	Journeys to Special Places	●						
	9	Lourdes			●				
	10	Special Places for Buddhists		●					

Songs

If you have *Sounds of Music* in your school, you may like to use these songs to support your RE teaching.

Sounds of Music song	SoM year	Sounds of Music song	SoM year
Alleluia	Y5/P6	I'm Gonna Sing	Y3/P4
Animals	Y2/P3	In the Summertime	Y1/P2
Autumn Leaves	Y1/P2	Join in the Game	Y1/P2
Away in a Manger	N&R/P1	Kite Song	Y4/P5
Baby Lying in a Manger	Y1/P2	Lazy Summertime	Y3/P4
Busy Farmer, The	Y1/P2	Lord of all Hopefulness	Y4/P5
Chanukah Song	Y2/P3	Now Light 1000 Christmas Lights	Y6/P7
Christmas is Coming	Y5/P6	Pinata Song	Y4/P5
Come and Sing	Y2/P3	Polish the Old Menorah	Y6/P7
Crossing the River	Y2/P3	Posada Song	Y2/P3
Dayenu	Y5/P6	Quietly	Y3/P4
Divali Song	Y6/P7	River, River	Y3/P4
Easter Bunny Hop	Y1/P2	Shadow Song	Y3/P4
Eternal Father	Y5/P6	Sing for Joy	Y4/P5
Evening Prayer	Y3/P4	Sing One Song	Y2/P3
First Nowell, The	Y5/P6	Sing Some Happy Song	Y4/P5
Five Angels	N&R/P1	Song of Thanks	Y1/P2
Floating in Space	Y4/P5	Sowing and Reaping	Y1/P2
Good Morning	Y1/P2	Thanks for Life	Y4/P5
Greensleeves	Y4/P5	Vesper Hymn	Y5/P6
Ha Sukkah	Y1/P2	When you Live in a Lighthouse	Y5/P6
Hark the Herald Angels Sing	Y5/P6	Winter Lullaby	Y1/P2
Here We Go Santy Maloney	Y1/P2	Winter Now is Gone	Y3/P4
I Saw Three Ships	Y2/P3	World Keeps Turning Around, The	Y5/P6

Sounds of Music is Stanley Thornes' primary CD-based music scheme which offers structured year-on-year progression from Nursery and Reception/P1 through to Year 6/P7. Clearly organised with comprehensive teacher support and specific help with planning, assessment and differentiation, *Sounds of Music* makes music straightforward to teach, whatever your own musical expertise.

For details please contact
Stanley Thornes Primary Customer Services, Ellenborough House, Wellington Street, Cheltenham, GL50 1YW,
telephone 01242 577944/228888, fax 01242 253695

infant RE

Class Record Sheet Unit ....

Teacher .... Class .... Date ....

Lesson	Religious focus	Learning about religion	Learning from religion
1			
2			
3			
4			
5			
6			
7			
8			
9			
10			

This record sheet is designed for brief notes on opportunities for children's learning which have been developed during each Unit.